C000233726

COVENTRY CITY
On This Day

COVENTRY CITY
On This Day

*History, Facts & Figures
from Every Day of the Year*

STEVE PHELPS

COVENTRY CITY
On This Day

History, Facts & Figures from Every Day of the Year

All statistics, facts and figures are correct as of 1st August 2010

© Steve Phelps

Steve Phelps has asserted his rights in accordance with the Copyright, Designs and Patents Act 1988 to be identified as the author of this work.

Published By:
Pitch Publishing (Brighton) Ltd
A2 Yeoman Gate
Yeoman Way
Durrington
BN13 3QZ

Email: info@pitchpublishing.co.uk
Web: www.pitchpublishing.co.uk

First published 2010

A catalogue record for this book is available from the British Library.

ISBN: 978-1-9054118-8-7

Printed and bound in Malta by Gutenburg Press

This book is for my wife, Emma, and our five-year-old daughters, Aimee and Jolie.

ACKNOWLEDGEMENTS

I'd like to thank a number of people for their assistance with this project. Bobby Gould for kindly supplying the foreword, and for taking the time to share his many memories of Coventry City Football Club. Jim Brown for his invaluable reference sources, *Coventry City The Elite Era*, *Coventry City: A Complete Record 1883-1991* written with Rod Dean, David Brassington and Don Chalk, *Coventry City: The Seven-Year Itch 2001-2008* and for helping me with the odd gap that arose.

Carl Newell, publications editor at Coventry City Football Club, for supplying the pictures for this book and David Antill for pointing me in Carl's direction. Thanks also to Pitch Publishing and commissioning editor Dan Tester for their professionalism and expertise to produce such a fantastic book to add to their established On This Day series. To Emma for her patience and encouragement, we can have conversations again now. And to my Dad, Rich, Steve Hewins and Ade Watts for sharing their sky-blue memories.

FOREWORD BY BOBBY GOULD

What an honour and a pleasure to be asked to write the foreword for *Coventry City: On This Day,* my beloved club. When I say 'my' I must remind you I've been supporter, player and twice manager of this great football club!

As a supporter I was taken to Highfield Road by my Granddad, Dickie Gould, a season ticket holder in the then South Stand in season 1953/54. Each home game saw me buy a cushion to sit on (bench seats only in those days) to watch my new heroes Reg Matthews, Roy Kirk, Ian Jamieson (my chairman in 1983), Eddie Brown, Frank Austin and flying winger Gordon Nutt.

Half-time meant a meat pie then when the whistle blew it was home to Forknell Avenue and down to the newsagents to collect *The Pink.* From 1955 through to 1961 I was allowed to venture out to matches on my own, or with my best mate Terry Clarke, who I first met at Stoke Council Juniors and we then moved to Caludon Castle School together. Football was our love, through good and bad times, our viewing point was the Spion Kop or just behind the goal where our new hero, Arthur Lightening, wore the number one shirt. Other stars for us were Ray Straw, Lol Harvey, Peter Hill and Ray Sambrook.

I left school at 15 and, having played for Coventry Schoolboys and scored a few goals, was invited to Coventry City for trials. Alas, eight weeks later, manager Billy Frith said three damaging words, "not enough pace" and I was on my way. Ronnie Rees put his arm around my shoulder and said "you'll be back one day". Fast forward to the Kings Lynn defeat. Jimmy Hill asked me back for a trial, I played well and was invited back! The rest is history, the Sky Blue wagon rolled on and we all know what happened... or do we?

What happened prior to my first visit to Highfield Road and what happened after I left? When did I become manager? Did I come back for more? When did I debut for my hometown club? It's all in here so read on and keep turning the pages that define Sky Blue activity on every day of the year....

Bobby Gould

INTRODUCTION

Coventry City On This Day covers Sky Blue activity on every day of the year and documents events in the club's history from the day it was founded, Monday 13th August 1883, right through to Aidy Boothroyd's recent appointment at the Ricoh Arena.

From Terry Butcher's final game in charge to Jimmy Hill's promotion chasing side's 5-1 victory over Portsmouth, the memories are endless as you turn the pages. The many highs and lows are detailed in the calendar year and provide fascinating reading.

January and February see either cup shocks or cup runs as winter kicks in. March is make or break for promotion pushes and those cup quarter-finals as Wembley looms on the horizon. April and May conclude with promotions, relegations and glorious days out at Wembley. World Cups and European Championships take the summer focus, while the revolving door welcomes new and says goodbye to old. There's Sky Blue optimism as the fixtures are released and the new season dawns. European competition commences along with League Cup first- and second-leg ties. As the nights draw in, the fixtures come thick and fast; the draw is made for the FA Cup third round as the festive season draws closer. It's all in here, a daily account of an amazing football club.

A day-by-day account of happenings at Coventry City cannot cover everything but the contents of this book highlight just what a great club we support. The time spent compiling this book has been extremely enjoyable and each page is crammed with facts and figures of sky blue interest.

As Aidy Boothroyd commented to the *Coventry Evening Telegraph* days into his tenure, "I think we have got something really, really good here – and it's just starting!"

Steve Phelps

COVENTRY CITY
On This Day

JANUARY

WEDNESDAY 1st JANUARY 1992

Terry Butcher's final match as manager of Coventry ended in a 2-1 defeat to Tottenham Hotspur at Highfield Road. Paul Stewart added to Gary Lineker's equaliser to send City down to 15th in Division One after Robert Rosario had given City an early lead. Butcher went on to manage Sunderland, Motherwell, Sydney FC, Brentford and Inverness Caledonian Thistle, where he remains to this day.

MONDAY 1st JANUARY 2001

Right-back Marc Edworthy scored the Sky Blues' first goal of the year as they rescued a point in the home match against Manchester City. It would be the only goal Edworthy scored in sky blue during his four seasons at the club in which he made 85 first team appearances before moving on to Wolverhampton Wanderers.

MONDAY 2nd JANUARY 1978

A Charlie George hat-trick at the Baseball Ground ensured Derby County began 1978 with a 4-2 victory. Late goals from Mick Ferguson and Barry Powell gave the scoreline some respectability but it was too little too late as the Sky Blues dropped to seventh in the table. George signed for Coventry in the summer of 1983 but did not play a competitive game for the club.

SATURDAY 2nd JANUARY 1999

Macclesfield Town's FA Cup third round visit to Highfield Road saw Darren Huckerby collect the first of two successive match balls. The Sky Blues equalled their highest-ever FA Cup win with a 7-0 thrashing and the biggest home win for 35 years. Leeds United paid £5.5 million to take Huckerby to Elland Road the following summer.

FRIDAY 3rd JANUARY 1969

A creative midfielder with an excellent left foot, Chris Marsden was born in Sheffield. Signed on loan by Phil Neal, he dovetailed perfectly with Roy Wegerle and Peter Ndlovu as City entertained. When his loan period expired, Wolves signed him on a permanent deal as City missed their opportunity. He went on to play over 120 games for Southampton in the Premier League alongside Matt Le Tissier.

MONDAY 3RD JANUARY 1977

Youssef Safri, who played 98 times for Coventry City between 2001 and 2004, was born in Casablanca, Morocco. He made his debut as substitute in the 1-0 home defeat to Grimsby Town which signalled the departure of Gordon Strachan. His only goal came against Sheffield Wednesday in a 2-0 win when City topped the second tier for just four days.

SATURDAY 3RD JANUARY 1987

Seven days before City launched their famous cup run, St. James' Park witnessed the Sky Blues win 2-1 in front of 22,366 Geordies. Dave Bennett's first-minute strike may have had something to do with Brian Kilcline taking a wrong turn and leading the side out into the car park prior to kick off. Once the laughter subsided the win took City up to eighth place.

SATURDAY 3RD JANUARY 1998

Around 4,000 Sky Blues supporters witnessed City overturn an early Jamie Redknapp goal to win 3-1 at Anfield in the FA Cup third round. Darren Huckerby, Dion Dublin and Paul Telfer scored the goals to secure the unlikely triumph. Gordon Strachan, speaking to the *Daily Mirror*, summed up the jubilation: "All my players were terrific. When you come to Liverpool you expect a hard game and I didn't think we'd win and create so many chances."

SATURDAY 4TH JANUARY 1992

Division Two pacesetters Cambridge United brought their long-ball product to Highfield Road. A Brian Borrows penalty with 13 minutes remaining secured a replay at the Abbey Stadium after Dion Dublin had opened the scoring on the half hour. City lost the replay in injury time when Dublin followed up his penalty miss to bundle the ball into the net.

TUESDAY 4TH JANUARY 2005

Following a 2-1 home defeat to Leeds United, Peter Reid left the Sky Blues managerial hot seat after only eight months. Hired by chairman Mike McGinnity to be the 'high profile' figure the club needed, his objective was clear: 'instant success'. Eight wins in 28 games proved the final straw for the City board.

TUESDAY 5TH JANUARY 1965

Jose Perdomo, who made just four first-team appearances in season 1990-91, was born in Salto, Uruguay. As well as being unfit throughout his brief loan cameo, an outstanding passing display in the Rumbelows Cup tie against Bolton Wanderers at Highfield Road raised hopes he may sign permanently. His range of passing was unlike anything seen for many years but injuries saw him move to Real Betis, and then Penarol, before retiring in 1994. He won 27 caps for Uruguay and played in the 1990 World Cup finals.

SATURDAY 6TH JANUARY 1934

Arthur 'Rasher' Bacon replaced the injured Clarrie Bourton in the number nine shirt while City's all-time leading scorer recuperated. In just 21 first-team appearances he scored 19 goals. As well as sharing the all-time individual goal record of five with Cyrille Regis and Bourton, he added four to his total on this day as City beat Crystal Palace 5-1 at Highfield Road. He moved on in 1936 after suffering an eye injury and died in 1941, aged just 36.

FRIDAY 6TH JANUARY 1950

Willie Carr, who joined Coventry City as an apprentice in 1967, was born in Glasgow. He played 288 first-team games and scored 36 goals from his central midfield position. It was Carr's back flick that lifted the ball into the air for Ernie Hunt to volley into Everton's net, the 'donkey kick', which was later outlawed by the football authorities. While at City he collected six Scottish caps and then spent a further seven years at Wolverhampton Wanderers where he picked up a League Cup winners' medal in 1980.

SATURDAY 6TH JANUARY 1990

City travelled to Northampton Town's County Ground on a wet and windy FA Cup third round day. The Sky Blues were defeated by a Steve Berry goal just before half-time. Just three years after their Wembley appearance six of the cup-winning side took the field with Cyrille Regis named on the bench. Comedian Alan Carr's father, Graham, was the Cobblers' manager and would oversee relegation to Division Four the following season.

SATURDAY 7TH JANUARY 1984

City took three games to defeat Wolverhampton Wanderers in their FA Cup third-round tie. After two 1-1 draws, a 3-0 victory at Highfield Road took the Sky Blues into round four and a visit to Division Two Sheffield Wednesday. The first tie against Wolves captured the drama of the FA Cup. Referee John Martin awarded a highly controversial penalty when Sam Allardyce collided with Wayne Clarke. Prior to the kick, a City supporter ran onto the pitch from the Spion Kop and offered the hapless official his spectacles. Wayne Clarke's penalty was then saved by penalty specialist Raddy Avramovic to ensure a replay.

SATURDAY 7TH JANUARY 1989

Coventry's worst-ever result was broadcast to the nation as non-league part-timers Sutton United defeated the 1987 FA Cup winners 2-1. Sutton's opening goal was scored by captain Tony Rains. Speaking to *Match of the Day* he commented: "When you have something at stake that was that high for us, something that has only been achieved five or six other times in history, you do anything to hold onto it." David Phillips levelled the score and City fans breathed a sigh of relief until just six minutes later when Matthew Hanlon headed home to secure a fourth-round tie at Norwich City. Their trip to Carrow Road saw the Canaries win 8-0.

TUESDAY 8TH JANUARY 1974

Due to the national power crisis, City's FA Cup third-round replay against Sheffield Wednesday kicked off at 1.30pm in front of a crowd of just over 13,000. Goals from David Cross, Tommy Hutchison and a Mick Coop penalty took the side into the fourth round where they would defeat Derby County after a replay.

SATURDAY 8TH JANUARY 1983

The last non-league visitors to Highfield Road were Kings Lynn in 1961. After 18 minutes City trailed to a Paul Moss penalty as Worcester City silenced the 12,000 crowd in the third-round tie. The lead lasted for only 12 minutes as Steve Whitton levelled from the penalty spot and Mark Hateley added an immediate second. With five minutes remaining Whitton added a third to send City into round four.

SATURDAY 9TH JANUARY 1988

The FA Cup holders endured a nervous first hour against Fourth Division Torquay United in defence of their trophy. A crowd of 16,967 watched Brian Kilcline and Cyrille Regis send the Devon team back down the M5 with a 2-0 defeat. The only additions to the cup-winning side were Kevan Smith deputising for Trevor Peake at centre-half and David Speedie alongside Cyrille Regis in place of Keith Houchen.

SATURDAY 9TH JANUARY 1993

The original visit to Carrow Road was postponed due to freezing weather conditions in East Anglia. City, therefore, entered the fourth-round draw and travelled again four days later when Darren Beckford's 46th-minute goal divided the teams. Norwich embarked on a fine run which saw them end the season in third position in the Premier League. The Sky Blues had lost 5-0 at Old Trafford in their previous game and finished the season in 15th position.

SATURDAY 10TH JANUARY 1987

Little did Sky Blues' followers realise victory against Bolton Wanderers would be the start of the magical journey to Wembley. Bolton Wanderers manager Phil Neal publicly blamed goalkeeper Mike Salmon for all three first-half City goals in front of 12,051 supporters. Michael Gynn, with his low centre of gravity, starred in the match as Wanderers struggled with the icy conditions. Greg Downs' free kick was his first goal for the club and spawned the chant: "He's got no hair but we don't care, Greggy, Greggy Downs!"

SUNDAY 10TH JANUARY 1999

Darren Huckerby scored his second successive hat-trick in the Sky Blues' 4-0 demolition of struggling Nottingham Forest. Taking his tally for the season to ten, Huckerby was praised by skipper Gary McAllister. Speaking to the *Sunday Mirror*, Coventry's number ten said: "Darren can do anything he wants in this game. He is chasing the likes of Michael Owen and Robbie Fowler, with enough ability to think he might catch them one day. Darren just needs to be more consistent." Forest goalkeeper Dave Beasant said: "Our second half was the worst I have ever experienced. We made Coventry look like Brazil."

SATURDAY 11TH JANUARY 1908

The club's first official matchday programme was produced for the FA Cup first-round tie against Crystal Palace at Highfield Road which was lost 4-2.

MONDAY 11TH JANUARY 1971

Fourth Division Rochdale won 2-1 at Spotland on a Monday afternoon in front of 13,011 supporters in the FA Cup third round. David Cross, who joined the Sky Blues in 1973, scored the opening goal before Ernie Hunt levelled just after half-time. Rochdale's winner came in the 80th minute from Dennis Butler. When the draw was made, City manager Noel Cantwell commented: "Rochdale – where's that?"

FRIDAY 11TH JANUARY 1985

The Baseball Ground hosted the FA Cup third-round tie between Burton Albion and Leicester City. During the game, which Leicester won 6-1, Burton goalkeeper Paul Evans was struck by missiles from Leicester fans stood behind his goal. The Football Association ordered a replay behind closed doors at Highfield Road and Leicester won 1-0 with a goal from midfielder Paul Ramsey.

SATURDAY 11TH JANUARY 1992

Don Howe's first game in charge following Terry Butcher's sacking ended in a 2-2 draw with Queens Park Rangers at Highfield Road. Kevin Gallacher and Robert Rosario gave City a two-goal lead before Gary Penrice scored two goals in eight minutes to level matters.

SATURDAY 12TH JANUARY 1980

A 1-0 defeat at Norwich City saw City field seven players aged under 21. Ray Gooding, Paul Dyson, Gary Gillespie, Tommy English, Mark Hateley, Andy Blair and substitute Steve Whitton completed the game.

SATURDAY 13TH JANUARY 1973

Over 4,000 City supporters watched a comprehensive 4-1 FA Cup third-round win at Leyton Orient on a cold, wet afternoon at Brisbane Road. Two goals from Brian Alderson with one each from Willie Carr and Tommy Hutchison gave the Sky Blues an emphatic victory in a season where they would reach the quarter-final for only the third time ever.

THURSDAY 13TH JANUARY 2005

The club announced that the traditional badge would be replaced with an updated, modern version. This provoked a strong response from Sky Blues' supporters' groups and the plan was quickly revoked.

SATURDAY 13TH JANUARY 2007

Crystal Palace took a 4-0 lead after 39 minutes in Micky Adams' final Championship match as manager. Leon McKenzie and Kevin Kyle ensured the scoreline looked slightly better in the following morning's newspapers as City conceded from four crosses. A crowd of 16,582 had long turned for home before the final whistle shrilled. Carl Fletcher, Shefki Kuqi, Leon Cort and Jobi McAnuff benefited from the charitable defending in front of Luke Steele.

SATURDAY 14TH JANUARY 1984

Watford goalkeeper Steve Sherwood opened the scoring with a wind assisted drop kick at Highfield Road. Watford winger Nigel Callaghan challenged Avramovic to the bouncing ball, the City custodian missed his punch and the ball rolled into the unguarded net. Trevor Peake drew City level before George Reilly's header in stoppage time gave Watford the points. Back in 1984 goalkeepers did not venture up for last-minute corner kicks, or take penalty kicks, so this made Sherwood's only career goal all the more unique.

SATURDAY 15TH JANUARY 1972

Coventry's first away cup victory over a Division One side for 60 years was a long time in waiting. The Hawthorns always posed a tricky proposition for the Sky Blues and the record would take a turn for the worse in the late 1970s. Chris Chilton's late header saw the Sky Blues win 2-1 against an Albion side which featured Asa Hartford, Tony Brown, John Wile and former City striker Bobby Gould.

SATURDAY 15TH JANUARY 1983

Mark Hateley scored after just 14 seconds to give City the lead at Southampton. David Armstrong's equaliser took the Sky Blues up to fifth in the Division One table. The Saints side included Peter Shilton, Mick Mills, Mark Wright, Steve Moran and Danny Wallace.

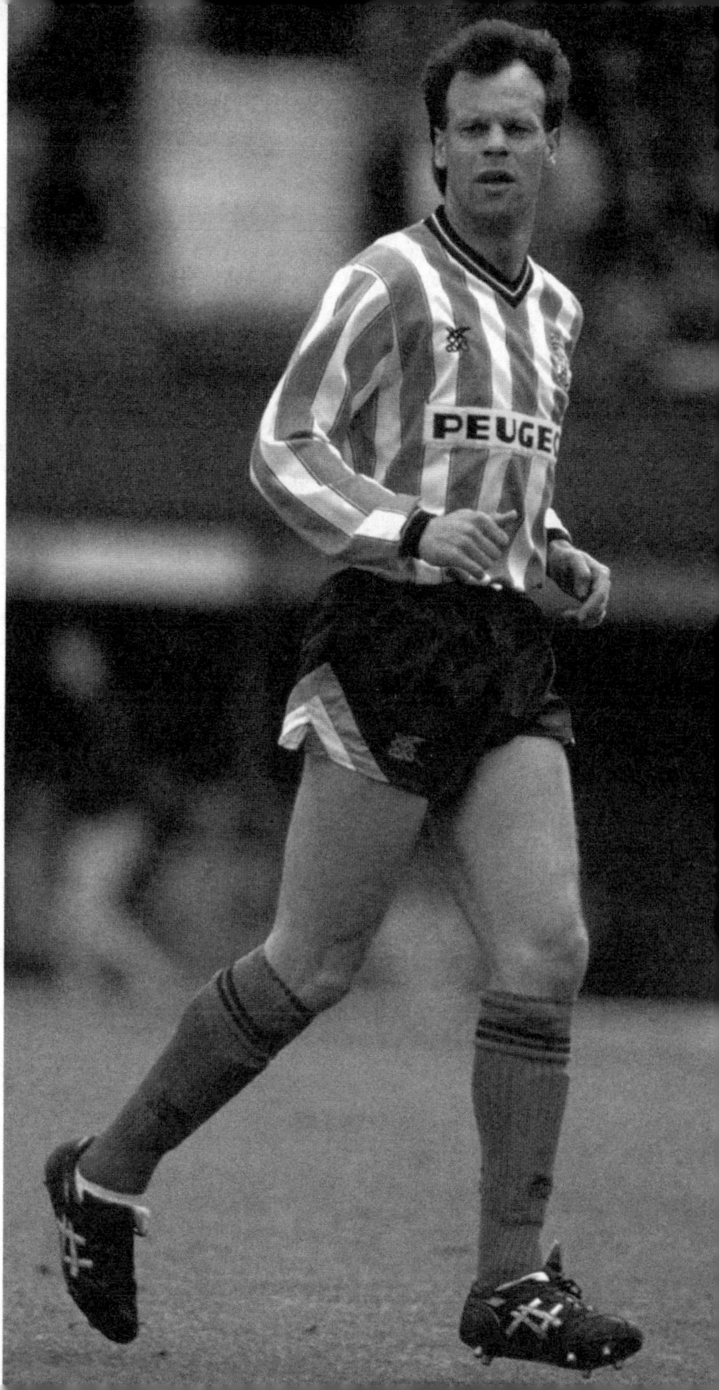

TREVOR PEAKE LEVELLED STEVE SHERWOOD'S FREAK GOAL

MONDAY 16TH JANUARY 1956

Martin Jol, who was outstanding on his home debut for Coventry against Norwich City in August 1984, was born in The Hague, Netherlands. He played just over a dozen first-team games before he returned to his home country and signed for Den Haag. The following season he won the Dutch Footballer of The Year award. After playing he moved into management, spending three seasons at Tottenham Hotspur, and is now manager of Ajax.

WEDNESDAY 16TH JANUARY 1974

City's League Cup quarter-final replay was preceded by a bomb hoax at Maine Road. The first game was played almost a month earlier with an afternoon kick off, due to the power crisis, and ended 2-2. In front of just over 25,000 fans, the Sky Blues led 2-1 with 23 minutes remaining. A late trio of goals from Francis Lee (2) and Denis Law took Manchester City into a semi-final with Plymouth Argyle. They would lose 2-1 to Wolverhampton Wanderers at Wembley in the final.

SATURDAY 16TH JANUARY 1982

Gerry Francis had joined City on loan and was instrumental in an excellent performance as City led Ipswich Town 2-1 with just over ten minutes remaining. When Francis was substituted due to injury, City fell to pieces and by 87 minutes were 4-2 down. Ipswich consolidated their position at the top of Division One with late goals from Arnold Muhren, Paul Mariner and Alan Brazil.

TUESDAY 16TH JANUARY 2007

Following the 3-3 FA Cup third-round draw at Ashton Gate the previous Saturday, City's travelling contingent chanted "See you at the Ricoh!", confident of progression into round four. Just over 13,000 fans, including 2,500 from the West Country, saw the visitors dominate from start to finish, deservedly winning 2-0. Goals from Scott Murray and Enoch Showumni gave the prelude for the "Adams Out" chants. Soon after the final whistle Micky Adams departed Coventry City. His final signing, Michael Mifsud, a Maltese international, would go on to write his own chapter in Sky Blue history the following season.

TUESDAY 17TH JANUARY 1978

Patrick Suffo, who collected a gold medal for Cameroon in the 2000 Olympics, was born in Ebolowa, Cameroon. He appeared in the 2002 World Cup, sent off in the final group game against Germany, and was signed by Gary McAllister in the summer of 2003. After just under 50 appearances and ten goals he departed for the Dubai Club in the summer of 2005 when his contract expired.

SATURDAY 17TH JANUARY 2004

Following Gary McAllister's resignation his assistant, Eric Black, took over as manager. His first game in charge saw City, backed by a large travelling support, beat Walsall 6-1 at the Bescot Stadium. Goals from Andy Morrell (2), Gary McSheffrey (2), Julian Joachim, and an own goal from City fan Ian Roper, equalled their best post-war away victory. McSheffrey even passed up a rare hat-trick opportunity when his late penalty rebounded back off a post.

THURSDAY 18TH JANUARY 1951

Bob Latchford, who scored City's opening goal in season 1984/85 in their third game, at home to Leicester City, was born in Birmingham. Signed by Bobby Gould he played alongside Terry Gibson in an all-too-brief Sky Blues career. In a dozen games Latchford netted one other goal in the 6-2 defeat to Chelsea at Stamford Bridge.

SATURDAY 18TH JANUARY 1986

Just 7,478 supporters turned out to watch Watford take the three points with a 2-0 victory at Highfield Road. Tony Coton seemed inspired every time he visited and today was no exception. John Barnes' double strike left the Sky Blues in 17th position. The attendance was the lowest since 1962 on a cold, winter afternoon.

SUNDAY 18TH JANUARY 1987

The *Big Match* cameras captured Coventry 'live' for the first time in a goalless draw at Highbury. With Arsenal top of the league, their attacking play sparkled and 19-year-old David Rocastle tormented Greg Downs with 90 minutes of trickery. Only 17,561 attended the game, the stadium half empty with the Gunners over 20 games unbeaten.

SATURDAY 19TH JANUARY 1980

Paul Dyson headed the only goal in a fantastic 1-0 win over reigning champions Liverpool. Their long unbeaten run came to an end as Dyson headed home after six minutes in front of 31,644 supporters. Dyson played nearly 150 games for City until he transferred to Stoke City in the infamous summer exodus of 1983. His partnership with Gary Gillespie had seen the pair progress through the youth ranks before both departed within weeks of each other. Dyson's move to Stoke would see him relegated with a then lowest-ever points tally for a top flight side in 1984.

SATURDAY 19TH JANUARY 1985

A 3-0 home defeat by Aston Villa was dominated by City's midland neighbours on the very day Elliott Ward was born in Harrow. Mark Walters tormented City down the Villa left wing and he notched a double along with Paul Rideout's header. Elliott Ward joined City from West Ham United in the summer of 2006. At the end of his four-year contract it appears likely he will leave the club. City supporters remember his vital series of penalty kicks that contrived to keep the side in the Championship at the end of season 2008. One memory he would not cherish is the penalty casually chipped straight into the arms of Southampton's Kelvin Davis during City's 4-1 win in October 2008.

SATURDAY 20TH JANUARY 1990

John Sillett's side conceded a late David White goal at Maine Road as Manchester City took three points which went some way to ensuring they finished level on points at the end of the season with neighbours United. Peter Reid, Colin Hendry and Ian Brightwell lined up for the hosts; all would feature for the Sky Blues in later years. Coventry ended the season in 12th position, one point and one place ahead of Alex Ferguson's Manchester United. Sillett's side comprised Steve Ogrizovic, Brian Borrows, Tony Dobson, Lloyd McGrath, Peter Billing, Trevor Peake, Michael Gynn, David Speedie, Cyrille Regis, Steve Livingstone and David Smith. Local lad Howard Clark replaced McGrath and went on to make 23 first-team appearances, mainly as substitute, scoring one goal.

SATURDAY 21st JANUARY 1989

One of the best goals seen at Highfield Road was afforded the 12,471 supporters who watched Coventry defeat Wimbledon's 'Crazy Gang' 2-1. David Speedie's left-foot chip over Hans Segers in front of the West Terrace was worth the admission alone. This followed a similarly exquisite piece of skill the previous Saturday at Carrow Road as the same player chipped Bryan Gunn with two minutes remaining to take the three points. Both games followed the Sutton United debacle and reminded City fans just how good their side and its players were.

SATURDAY 21st JANUARY 2006

Dennis Wise made his City debut against Derby County at The Ricoh Arena. He became the Sky Blues' oldest debutant at the age of 39, surpassing the 38-year-old Gordon Strachan. Having been an unpopular visitor to Highfield Road for many seasons, he took just eight seconds to warm the hearts of City followers with a robust challenge on Seth Johnson. His deflected drive looped over Derby goalkeeper, Lee Camp, after 59 minutes to extend the lead to 3-1. When Micky Adams substituted him with minutes to play a standing ovation was afforded. The last time City won 6-1 at home was back in 1982 when Sunderland visited.

SATURDAY 22nd JANUARY 1977

Self-proclaimed Bristol City supporter, Louis Carey, was signed by Peter Reid in the summer of 2004. Born in Bristol, Reid played the central defender as a right-back and appointed him City's corner taker on the left-hand side. Carey commuted in from Bristol every day and never settled. Upon Peter Reid's departure, Micky Adams agreed a return to Bristol City for Carey after just 27 first-team appearances. Since his return to Ashton Gate he recently clocked his 500th first-team appearance.

SATURDAY 22nd JANUARY 2000

City's last away win was the previous April when they travelled to Hillsborough and took the points with a late Noel Whelan goal. The 0-0 draw with Derby County at Pride Park saw a weakened Coventry side hold on for a point in the season where they would not win a single away game.

SATURDAY 23rd JANUARY 1982

Peter Bodak won the January Goal of the Month with the third goal in City's terrific 3-1 FA Cup fourth-round victory at Maine Road. He chipped the colossal Joe Corrigan from the edge of the penalty area to send the Sky Blues through to a fifth-round tie at home to Oxford United. Steve Hunt and Mark Hateley gave City a 2-0 lead after just 22 minutes before Kevin Bond replied with a penalty kick. Bodak's piece of magic saw him sprint onto a pass from Ian Butterworth, twenty yards inside his own half, and finish in style.

SATURDAY 23rd JANUARY 1999

Another Sky Blue FA Cup fourth-round away-day triumph, this time at Filbert Street, saw City into round five and an away trip to Everton. George Boateng saw red with City 1-0 ahead through a Noel Whelan strike. Matt Elliott then missed a penalty for the Foxes before Paul Telfer and Steve Froggatt raced away in added time to add further goals.

WEDNESDAY 24th JANUARY 1990

Steve Livingstone scored four times as City overcame Second Division Sunderland 5-0 to win the Rumbelows Cup quarter-final replay after a 0-0 draw at Roker Park. 'Livvo' had previously scored the winner in extra time to win the FA Youth Cup in May 1987 against Charlton Athletic. He would score in the semi-final first leg at the City Ground before a Stuart Pearce special gave Nottingham Forest a slender advantage that would take them to Wembley. In 1991, Kenny Dalglish signed Livingstone, along with Tony Dobson, for Blackburn Rovers. He later spent ten seasons with Grimsby Town before retiring in early 2004.

SATURDAY 25th JANUARY 1969

George Curtis made his 500th first-team appearance in the FA Cup fourth-round defeat to Everton at Goodison Park. A crowd of 53,289 saw the Toffees progress to the fifth round with goals from Joe Royle and John Hurst. City ended the season in 20th position, but with 22 teams in the division only the bottom two were relegated. They survived by a single point as Leicester City and Queens Park Rangers dropped into Division Two.

SATURDAY 25TH JANUARY 1997

Non-league Woking equalised in the 89th minute at Highfield Road as City were taken to a third-round replay. Eoin Jess had given City an undeserved lead in front of just 16,011 spectators. Gordon Strachan was livid after the game as he spoke to *The Independent*: "I've not spoken to the players because I wouldn't know where to begin. Our performance was indefensible. What happened will not be tolerated." City scraped into round four with a 2-1 win in the replay.

SATURDAY 25TH JANUARY 2003

FA Cup humiliation at Rochdale saw Gary McAllister's side defeated 2-0 at Spotland in round four. Rochdale goalscorer, centre-half Gareth Griffiths, summed up City's abject display to *The Independent*: "We expected them to cause us a few more problems. They were coming to a Third Division club but a few of them had an off day and a few of us rose to the challenge. That's the magic of the cup."

SATURDAY 26TH JANUARY 1980

Third Division Blackburn Rovers, managed by Howard Kendall, joined the growing band of January cup shockers with a 1-0 win at Ewood Park. A frozen pitch played havoc as Rovers scored on 29 minutes through much-travelled striker Andy Crawford.

SUNDAY 27TH JANUARY 1974

Coventry's first-ever Sunday game kicked off at 2.15pm with Derby County the visitors in front of a huge crowd of 41,281. The FA Cup fourth-round tie ended goalless and saw the Sky Blues win 1-0 after extra time in the replay at the Baseball Ground.

TUESDAY 27TH JANUARY 1981

With 35 minutes on the clock, West Ham led 2-0 in the first leg of the League Cup semi-final. Over 35,000 fans packed into Highfield Road to witness a superb second-half comeback as goals from Garry Thompson (2) and Gerry Daly hauled City into a first-leg advantage. Thompson had netted an own goal in the first half to claim an unlikely hat-trick and would leave City just 90 minutes from a first-ever Wembley appearance.

SATURDAY 28TH JANUARY 1956

City drew a crowd of 13,000 for a friendly visit of Division One Preston North End. Both City and Preston had a blank schedule as both were defeated in an earlier FA Cup round. The Coventry public caught a rare live glimpse of Tom Finney as he led North End to a 4-1 win.

WEDNESDAY 28TH JANUARY 1976

City crumbled 5-0 to Newcastle United in the FA Cup fourth-round replay at St. James' Park. Malcolm Macdonald scored twice along with Alan Gowling, Micky Burns and Tommy Cassidy as the Sky Blues failed to trouble the League Cup finalists.

FRIDAY 29TH JANUARY 1954

Barry Powell, who collected four under 23 caps for England, was born in Kenilworth. Powell joined Coventry in a swap deal involving Willie Carr who travelled to Wolverhampton Wanderers. He partnered Terry Yorath in the City midfield and would go on to make over 160 appearances between 1975 and 1979 before moving to Derby County for £350,000 in October 1979.

MONDAY 30TH JANUARY 1956

City played another friendly just two days after Preston's visit. San Lorenzo, a top Argentine side of the time, attracted a crowd of 17,000 on a wet and windy evening. The game was abandoned after 43 minutes. Top referee Arthur Ellis officiated and awarded a penalty just before half-time to the Sky Blues. This triggered madness amongst the San Lorenzo players. Midfielder Jose Sanfilippo kicked Ellis who duly sent him off. He refused to walk so both sides were ordered off the pitch and the game was abandoned.

SATURDAY 30TH JANUARY 1988

Highfield Road resembled Weston-super-Mare as the FA Cup holders relinquished their grip on the famous trophy. A Tony Coton-inspired Watford staged a smash and grab raid as lower league striking legend Trevor Senior took them into round five. The City team contained nine of Wembley's starting eleven but Coton's heroics left 22,366 supporters unable to believe the cup run was over.

SATURDAY 30TH JANUARY 1999

Victories against Liverpool were always treasured and this was no exception. Liverpool's 'Spice Boys' would finish the season in seventh place, ten away defeats a major factor. City's 2-1 victory at Highfield Road saw goals for George Boateng and Noel Whelan. Substitute Steve McManaman, roundly booed by the away support having just announced he would be leaving in the summer to join Real Madrid, pulled a goal back with four minutes remaining but the Sky Blues hung on to move up to 16th position.

SATURDAY 31st JANUARY 1987

The Twin Towers edged ever closer as a scrambled Keith Houchen goal gave City a 1-0 victory at Old Trafford on a freezing cold, icy day. The referee was Ray Lewis from Great Bookham who later on in the year would officiate the Charity Shield as Everton defeated the Sky Blues 1-0 in the annual curtain raiser. When the draw was made the following day, City prepared to head up the M6 as they were paired with Division Two side Stoke City at the Victoria Ground. Speaking to the *Daily Mirror*, Trevor Peake promised success to the supporters: "You ain't seen nothing yet, we can go on and win the FA Cup after that." Keith Houchen was equally jubilant: "I had at least three goes at it before it finally went in the net."

SATURDAY 31st JANUARY 1998

Coventry visited the Reebok Stadium for the first time as they thrashed Bolton Wanderers 5-1. Bolton were relegated four months later and results like this failed to assist them in their bid for survival. Left-back David Burrows praised Gordon Strachan as he spoke to the *Daily Mirror*: "This is the most settled and best bunch of lads I have ever seen at the club. Gordon Strachan has done an unbelievable job with these players. We are a completely different side to the one we were last year." Doubles from Darren Huckerby and Dion Dublin added to Noel Whelan's opener after Scott Sellars levelled. City ran riot in the second half to move up to 13th place as this victory marked the start of seven straight wins, a club record.

COVENTRY CITY
On This Day

FEBRUARY

SUNDAY 1st FEBRUARY 1959

Dave Bamber, who joined the Sky Blues in the summer of 1983, was born in Prescot, Merseyside. He began the season as Terry Gibson's strike partner yet his stay at Highfield Road was short-lived as he transferred to Walsall after just 22 first-team games during which time he scored four goals. Bamber went on to make over 400 appearances for a host of lower division sides.

FRIDAY 2nd FEBRUARY 1898

The Sky Blues appointed Harry Storer as manager in June 1931. Born in West Derby, Liverpool, Storer steered the club to the Division Three (South) championship in 1935/36 and left in 1945 to join Birmingham City. He returned to Highfield Road in 1948 for a further five years and departed in December 1953. Between 1920 and 1936 he also played cricket for Derbyshire. He sadly died on September 1st 1967.

WEDNESDAY 2nd FEBRUARY 1955

Jim Blyth, whose proposed £440,000 transfer to Manchester United would have made him the world's most expensive goalkeeper, was born in Perth, Scotland. Blyth appeared between 1972 and 1982 playing 151 first-team games. He left for Birmingham City in 1982 and retired in 1986 after further back problems which had scuppered his move to Old Trafford. A part of Gordon Strachan's management team, Blyth coached the goalkeepers at City, Southampton and Celtic. Two Scotland caps took him to the 1978 World Cup where he was second choice to Alan Rough.

SATURDAY 2nd FEBRUARY 1991

Lee Hurst and Terry Fleming made their debuts as City old boy Terry Gibson scored to give Wimbledon a 1-0 win at Plough Lane. Hurst went on to play just under 50 games for the side and starred in the inaugural Premier League season as he made 36 first-team appearances. A knee injury suffered on a pre-season training camp led to his premature retirement in 1996, aged just 26. Terry Fleming came through the youth ranks and featured in seasons 1991-93. He left for Northampton Town and carved out a career in the lower divisions, appearing over 450 times for a number of clubs.

FRIDAY 3RD FEBRUARY 1967

Former assistant manager and player Tim Flowers was born in Kenilworth, Warwickshire. As a player, Flowers realised a boyhood dream when he made his debut at Highfield Road in a 2-1 win over Walsall whilst on loan from Leicester City in 2002. He played five games while Magnus Hedman was injured and all three at Highfield Road resulted in victories. City supporter Flowers rejoined as part of Iain Dowie's managerial team in 2007 but departed when Dowie was sacked in February 2008.

FRIDAY 4TH FEBRUARY 1955

Gary Collier, who was the first-ever British footballer to move clubs through freedom of contract, was born in Bristol. Signed by Gordon Milne for £325,000 in the summer of 1979, Collier played just two first-team games, an opening-day 3-2 defeat at Stoke and a 4-0 defeat at Anfield. A centre-half, he was dropped and replaced by Gary Gillespie. US side Portland Timbers bought him for £365,000 just seven months later where he has remained to this day.

SATURDAY 4TH FEBRUARY 1984

When Jason Dozzell scored Ipswich Town's third goal in their victory over the Sky Blues, he became the youngest-ever Division One goalscorer. Aged just 16 years and 57 days, he came on as substitute for Eric Gates. Ipswich raced into a two-goal lead through Paul Mariner and Mark Brennan. Terry Gibson offered City hope until Dozzell's record-breaking moment in the 89th minute.

SATURDAY 5TH FEBRUARY 1972

Hull City visited Highfield Road in the FA Cup fourth round. In 2009, Hull supporters named Ken Wagstaffe their greatest-ever player. He netted after 77 minutes to silence over 24,000 supporters and joined the list of humiliations inflicted on Sky Blues supporters.

TUESDAY 5TH FEBRUARY 1974

Only 21,106 turned up at Anfield to watch Liverpool beat Coventry 2-1. The reason for the low crowd was the national power crisis. Played on a Tuesday afternoon before darkness set in, Kevin Keegan and Alec Lindsay scored for the Reds, Jimmy Holmes with City's consolation.

THURSDAY 5TH FEBRUARY 1976

Signed by Gordon Strachan from Portsmouth in December 1998, John Aloisi was born in Adelaide, Australia. He is well remembered for scoring two goals at Villa Park on the day City finally won a league game against Aston Villa on their home ground. After leaving post-relegation he played in Spain with Osasuna for four seasons and then went back to his native Australia.

SATURDAY 5TH FEBRUARY 2005

Micky Adams' first game in charge saw Coventry lose 3-2 at Preston North End. City supporter Graham Alexander, Richard Cresswell and Chris Lucketti scored the Preston goals, Claus Jorgensen and another City fan, Gary McSheffrey, replied for City. The Sky Blues' team that day comprised: Luke Steele, Andrew Whing, Richard Duffy, Richard Shaw, Ade Williams, Dean Leacock, Claus Jorgensen, Stephen Hughes, Dele Adebola, Gary McSheffrey and Michael Doyle. The substitutes were Graham Barrett and Neil Wood. Wood signed from Manchester United reserves on a season-long loan. He featured sporadically and went back to Old Trafford at the end of his loan period.

SATURDAY 6TH FEBRUARY 1932

Clarrie Bourton, the greatest goal scorer in the club's history, added a hat-trick to his eventual tally of 49 league goals as City destroyed Crystal Palace 8-0 at Highfield Road. Bourton and Jock Lauderdale's contribution saw the Sky Blues score 107 goals in season 1931/32.

SATURDAY 6TH FEBRUARY 1988

Manchester United supporters gave Sky Blues' followers a standing ovation in appreciation of a superbly respected minute's silence to commemorate the 30th anniversary of the Munich disaster. The 37,144 fans inside Old Trafford saw Liam O'Brien's fourth-minute goal take the points. David Smith came on as substitute for David Phillips to make his Coventry debut.

SATURDAY 7TH FEBRUARY 1981

Wolverhampton Wanderers clawed back a two-goal half-time deficit to take a share of the spoils at Highfield Road. Steve Hunt and Mark Hateley scored for the Sky Blues, John Richards and Sky Sports' very own Andy Gray ensured parity.

SKY BLUES LEGEND CYRILLE REGIS WAS BORN ON THIS DAY

THURSDAY 8TH FEBRUARY 1962

A prolific non-league marksman with Nuneaton Borough, Paul Culpin was born in Kirby Muxloe, Leicestershire. Signed by John Sillett and George Curtis in September 1985 he made his debut as substitute in a 5-2 home win over Oxford United. Eleven days later he opened the scoring at Villa Park in his first full game in Division One. He made only five first-team appearances before he was sold to Northampton Town in October 1987.

FRIDAY 8TH FEBRUARY 1980

Former Sky Blues captain, Stephen Wright, was born in Bootle, Liverpool. He joined on a two-year contract a day prior to the start of season 2008/09 having been released by Sunderland after six seasons. His career began at Liverpool, appearing just over 20 times in five seasons.

SUNDAY 9TH FEBRUARY 1958

Cyrille Regis, who led the City forward line between 1984 and 1991, was born in Maripasoula, French Guiana. Regis made 281 first-team appearances and scored 62 goals. His great strength and unselfish awareness made him a terrific focal point and all Coventry attacks came through him. Signed from West Bromwich Albion by Bobby Gould in 1984, it was when John Sillett took over that City supporters saw the best of Big Cyrille. It was a sad day when Terry Butcher released him in the summer of 1991 and he took the opportunity to sign for local rivals Aston Villa to reunite with Ron Atkinson. Wolverhampton Wanderers, Wycombe Wanderers and Chester City also benefited from the genius of Big Cyrille before his retirement.

SATURDAY 9TH FEBRUARY 2002

Coventry's biggest away win for 43 years came at Gresty Road, home of Crewe Alexandra. The 6-1 victory took the Sky Blues up to sixth position and raised hopes of an immediate return to the Premier League. Lee Hughes scored a hat-trick along with Laurent Delorge (two) and David Thompson completing the scoring. Valentine's Day 1959 at Brunton Park saw Billy Frith's side triumph by the same scoreline when George Stewart scored four times along with Ray Straw and Alan Daley.

TUESDAY 9TH FEBRUARY 2010

Referee Amy Fearn became the first woman to take charge of a Football League match. Fearn replaced injured Tony Bates after 70 minutes of Coventry's 1-0 win over Nottingham Forest. Her calm display impressed the watching crowd and afterwards she spoke to *Mirror Football*: "I understand there was a big reaction from the crowd but I don't remember it at the time. I'm glad there was nothing controversial in that 20 minutes, football should be about the players not the officials."

SUNDAY 10TH FEBRUARY 1957

With 334 first-team appearances for the Sky Blues between 1983 and 1991, Trevor Peake was one of the FA Cup-winning team. Peake, who was signed by Bobby Gould and made his debut at White Hart Lane in a 1-1 draw, was born in Nuneaton. His final City appearance in a 5-0 victory over Luton Town saw striker Sean Farrell sent off for elbowing him. Three days later Peake joined Luton Town where he played until his retirement in 1998. As part of City's defence, Peake and Brian Kilcline were one of the most popular central defensive pairings of all time.

TUESDAY 10TH FEBRUARY 1981

West Ham United turned the League Cup semi-final second leg on its head with a Paul Goddard equaliser before Jimmy Neighbour scored in the 89th minute to send West Ham into the final. Speaking to the *Daily Mirror*, City manager Gordon Milne expressed his disappointment: "West Ham thoroughly deserved their win – the better side got through. It is the worst we have played during our League Cup run. We never strung two passes together. I was disappointed to go out like we did."

SUNDAY 11TH FEBRUARY 1990

City appeared live on ITV for their Littlewoods Cup semi-final first leg at Nottingham Forest. Around 7,000 Sky Blues followers made the trip to the City Ground in driving rain to see City trail 2-1 at the halfway point in the tie. A superb Stuart Pearce free kick gave Forest the edge after Steve Livingstone had levelled Nigel Clough's first-half penalty. "You'll never beat Des Walker" rang out from the terraces as Forest hung on to a slender victory.

SATURDAY 11TH FEBRUARY 1995

A 2-0 win at Crystal Palace proved to be Phil Neal's last match in charge as manager. Late goals from Cobi Jones and Dion Dublin took City up three places to 17th position in the Premier League. Neal had been in charge for just under 18 months having taken over from Bobby Gould.

MONDAY 11TH FEBRUARY 2008

Iain Dowie and Tim Flowers were released from their contracts as manager and assistant manager, respectively. They joined in February 2007 and initial results were encouraging. A year later, the club was in a similar position and new chairman Ray Ranson felt the time was right for change as he spoke to *BBC Sport*: "We did not share the same ideals for the club. I felt that to move Coventry City forward towards a more progressive style of operating, I would need a different style of first-team management here."

THURSDAY 12TH FEBRUARY 1959

Mick Harford – who played only 11 minutes for Coventry yet managed to score the winner against Newcastle United at Highfield Road in August 1993 – was born in Sunderland. On as substitute for Tony Sheridan, Harford looped a far post header back across a despairing Tommy Wright to send the West Terrace delirious. Shortly afterwards, he picked up a back injury which ensured he would never play for the club again.

MONDAY 12TH FEBRUARY 2001

John Hartson made his Coventry debut at West Ham United in a 1-1 draw. With the Sky Blues in 19th position, Hartson scored six goals in 12 games to give the club a glimmer of hope. Three defeats out of the last four games saw the inevitable occur. Hartson was appointed captain by Gordon Strachan for City's assault on League Division One but departed for Celtic before the season got under way.

MONDAY 13TH FEBRUARY 1928

The club's worst-ever league attendance of 2,059 witnessed the visit of Crystal Palace. The Division Three (South) match under manager James Kerr ended in a 2-2 draw as the Bantams finished the season in 20th position.

SATURDAY 13TH FEBRUARY 1988

One of the best-ever full debuts by a Coventry player was given by David Smith. Out on the left side of midfield he tormented Sheffield Wednesday's England international Mel Sterland with a superb display. Not many players got the better of Sterland, yet Smith's performance was full of pace and trickery. He went on to play over 150 games for the Sky Blues yet never quite fulfilled his early promise. Birmingham City signed him in 1993, a spell at West Bromwich Albion followed before he ended his career with four seasons at Grimsby Town.

SATURDAY 14TH FEBRUARY 1987

There have not been many more endearing sights than the day Lloyd McGrath scored his first-ever Sky Blues goal. As McGrath's left-foot volley hit the Chelsea net from outside the penalty area, the roar was something to behold. One of the most popular players ever to represent the club, he went on to score again in the next home game against Sheffield Wednesday. City defeated Chelsea 3-0 with McGrath scoring the second in the 42nd minute. The win took them up to eighth place in Division One.

SATURDAY 14TH FEBRUARY 1998

For the first time ever, Coventry City won at Villa Park. The added bonus of an FA Cup quarter-final place was reward for a 1-0 victory which ensured this would be a day to remember. Romanian striker Viorel Moldovan scored only two goals in his brief stay at the club before he moved to Fenerbahce after the 1998 World Cup. His goal on 72 minutes ensured him a place in Sky Blue history.

WEDNESDAY 15TH FEBRUARY 1967

Gordon Strachan signed Trond Egil Soltvedt in the summer of 1997 from Norwegian champions Rosenborg. Born in Voss, Norway on this day, Soltvedt struggled to adapt to the pace of the Premiership initially then flourished as City finished in 11th position in his debut season. The arrival of Moustapha Hadji and Youssef Chippo invited Southampton to pay £300,000 for his midfield skills. He moved on to Sheffield Wednesday where he ended his English playing career before moving back to his native Norway.

MONDAY 16TH FEBRUARY 1976

Born on this day, Keith O'Neill signed from Middlesbrough post relegation for £750,000 in the Bryan Richardson spending era. His debut season saw him start the first five matches and then vanish from sight. His second season saw him fail to appear at all. The third and final season he appeared as substitute in a 3-1 home defeat to Nottingham Forest in August 2003. He replaced Michael Doyle then pulled a hamstring just eight minutes later. O'Neill was never seen again at Highfield Road, or any other football ground, and he retired with a parting shot as he spoke to *When Saturday Comes*: "I feel robbed of my best footballing years but I have been lucky enough to live out a dream for the last ten."

TUESDAY 16TH FEBRUARY 1982

Can you ever remember losing 5-1 at home with the opposition having three goals ruled out for offside? It happened on this day as Notts County won 5-1 at Highfield Road on a cold February evening in front of just 10,237 supporters. Newly promoted to Division One, County would finish the season just one place beneath the Sky Blues in 15th.

SUNDAY 16TH FEBRUARY 1986

Highfield Road witnessed a classic as City came from 2-0, 3-2 and 4-2 down to draw 4-4 with Birmingham City. Doubles from Dave Bennett and Brian Kilcline ensured the Sky Blues stayed in 16th position as 14,353 watched a superb end-to-end game of football. Future City chairman, Ray Ranson, lined up for Birmingham and was adjudged to have fouled Nick Pickering for Kilcline's 88th-minute leveller.

WEDNESDAY 17TH FEBRUARY 2010

The Sky Blues travelled to leaders Newcastle United on the back of a five-match unbeaten run which had taken them up to 11th in the Championship table. There was early optimism as Clinton Morrison swept City into an early lead but the side expected to secure automatic promotion back to the top flight hit back with four goals to give the scoreline a slightly flattering look. Goals from Routledge, Carroll, Lovenkrands and Ryan Taylor moved Newcastle three points clear of West Bromwich Albion.

SATURDAY 18TH FEBRUARY 1995

'Big Ron' Atkinson's first game as manager of Coventry saw the attendance rise from just under 13,500 for the previous home game to 17,563 for the visit of West Ham United. Atkinson's arrival saw the side stay unbeaten for six matches and gave fans the belief that he really could effect change at the football club. Peter Ndlovu and Mike Marsh scored the goals in a 2-0 win at Highfield Road.

SATURDAY 19TH FEBRUARY 1977

Prior to Christmas, striker Ian Wallace was injured in a car crash and hospitalised. His comeback at Carrow Road ended after only 12 minutes. Carried off on a stretcher, he had taken the ball full in the eye and returned to the casualty ward as City lost 3-0.

TUESDAY 19TH FEBRUARY 2008

Just eight days after Iain Dowie's departure, Chris Coleman took over as Coventry's new manager. Speaking to *BBC Sport* he said: "This is a big club, all geared to be in the Premier League. It will not be easy, but we want to build a team in order to do that. The most important thing for me is where the club wanted to be in a few years' time, and that is the Premier League." Sky Blues chairman, Ray Ranson said, "There are no quick fixes in football – we have got a five-year plan. Chris buys into that and I buy into what he hopes to achieve."

SATURDAY 20TH FEBRUARY 1960

David Speedie, who joined Coventry from Chelsea for £780,000 in the summer of 1987, was born in Glenrothes, Scotland. Signed by John Sillett, he made his debut in the Charity Shield defeat to Everton but scored on his league debut against Tottenham Hotspur the following week. His signature inspired this quote from John Sillett in the *Coventry Evening Telegraph*: "For too long this club has shopped at Woolworths, from now on, we'll be shopping at Harrods." He appeared 145 times for the Sky Blues and scored 35 goals in his four seasons at Coventry before Kenny Dalglish signed him for Liverpool.

SATURDAY 21st FEBRUARY 1942

Highfield Road suffered major bomb damage following three stray bombs which destroyed Coventry on the evening of November 14th 1940. It took 15 months for the Bantams (as City were named then) to play their next match, a friendly against a side representing the Czech Army at Coundon Road. It was the first match the club had played since 1940 and it would be a further three months before Highfield Road would host its first game since the outbreak of war.

SATURDAY 21st FEBRUARY 1987

The Victoria Ground, home of Stoke City, hosted the FA Cup fifth-round tie with 31,255 present, 8,000 from the West Midlands. Michael Gynn fired home a low shot with 19 minutes remaining in front of the sky blue masses to send City into the quarter-final. Cup fever gripped the city of Coventry and the quarter-final draw the following Monday lunchtime at 12.30pm on Radio 5 was eagerly anticipated.

SUNDAY 22nd FEBRUARY 1953

David Bradford, who signed from Washington Diplomats in 1981, was born in Manchester. He would play only seven first-team games for the Sky Blues having played for Blackburn Rovers and Sheffield United prior to moving to the USA to play in the North American Soccer League. His one goal for the club came in a 3-0 home victory over Stoke City. Speaking to the *Coventry Evening Telegraph* in 2005, he looked back over this moment: "I'd rate that goal as the best of my career, and it was my first in English football for six years."

THURSDAY 22nd FEBRUARY 1979

Three goals in five minutes saw the Sky Blues to a 3-1 win at Stamford Bridge. Ian Wallace and Mick Ferguson (two) took the side up to eighth in Division One and provoked a stern response from Chelsea manager Danny Blanchflower. Speaking to the *Daily Mirror* he retorted: "We lost it in those five minutes. It's disappointing because for half an hour we looked good. Coventry were effective, crude and tough, and in my opinion Jim Holton was guilty of blatant fouls every five minutes."

SATURDAY 22ND FEBRUARY 1986

With no home win since a 3-0 victory against rivals Leicester City at the start of October, the odds on the run ending looked bleak after 38 minutes. Southampton strolled into a two-goal lead courtesy of Mark Wright and a Glenn Cockerill penalty. Enter Dave Bennett to score the winner after setting up Nick Pickering and Alan Brazil to level at 2-2.

SATURDAY 23RD FEBRUARY 1985

With hooliganism high on some supporters' agenda, the visit of Chelsea and their infamous 'Headhunters' led to the match deemed 'all ticket' with the kick-off brought forward to 11.30am. Only 11,421 supporters watched City catch everyone out with Terry Gibson's winning goal after just two minutes. Lining up for the visitors as part of their deadly spearhead was David Speedie. His partnership with Kerry Dixon brought goals galore before John Sillett signed him for the Sky Blues.

WEDNESDAY 24TH FEBRUARY 1965

Lloyd McGrath, who played for Coventry between 1984 and 1994, was born in Birmingham. He progressed through the youth system before his debut came at Southampton in the infamous 8-2 drubbing. A 'ball winner', he gave the ball to others to create and mastermind attacks. Never afraid to put his body on the line, McGrath paid the price for his bravery with a broken leg against Ipswich in the Simod Cup. In 1987, his foray down the right wing and subsequent cross deflected in by Gary Mabbutt, earned him a place in Sky Blue folklore. Detailed to mark Glenn Hoddle, he did so with such style and aplomb that John Sillett was moved to comment to the *Daily Mail*: "Glenn Hoddle now knows all about Lloyd McGrath."

WEDNESDAY 25TH FEBRUARY 1970

Shaun Goater, who appeared six times for the Sky Blues prior to their departure from Highfield Road, was born in Hamilton, Bermuda. Signed by Micky Adams he failed to score during his short stay and was either substituted or a substitute. Prior to joining from Reading he had scarcely played and his match sharpness was lacking during his stay.

SUNDAY 25TH FEBRUARY 1973

Peter Ndlovu, who joined the Sky Blues in the summer of 1991 from Highlanders in Zimbabwe, was born in Bulawayo, Rhodesia (as it was then). Ndlovu would play 197 games with a return of 41 goals, during his six seasons with the club. Vital goals came his way over the years, none more so than the two he netted at Selhurst Park against Wimbledon that helped to stave off relegation fears. A hat-trick at Anfield also lined his CV, a feat only equalled by Andrei Arshavin in 2009 for Arsenal. 'Nuddy' as he was fondly known, played his final Sky Blues game in the vital 2-1 victory at Tottenham Hotspur in May 1997.

SUNDAY 25TH FEBRUARY 1990

The television cameras were again present for the second leg of the Littlewoods Cup semi-final as Nottingham Forest came to Highfield Road with a 2-1 lead. John Sillett's men never did manage to beat Des Walker, Stuart Pearce and company as 25,500 saw City lose 2-1 on aggregate after playing out a goalless draw. Forest would go on to beat Oldham Athletic 1-0 at Wembley in the final with a goal by future City loanee Nigel Jemson.

MONDAY 26TH FEBRUARY 1979

Signed on loan from VFL Bochum in 2004, Bjarni Gudjonsson made his debut in a 1-1 draw at home to Colchester United in the FA Cup fourth round. Born in Akranes, Iceland and signed by Eric Black, Gudjonsson starred in the wonderful attacking football that Black brought to Coventry. He signed permanently prior to Black's sacking but fell out of favour under Peter Reid and by October 2004 had played his last game.

SATURDAY 26TH FEBRUARY 2005

City's 0-0 draw with Stoke City proved far more eventful than the scoreline suggested. On loan City goalkeeper, Ian Bennett, became the first-ever Coventry goalkeeper to be sent off in a home match. Skipper Stephen Hughes took over in goal and produced a fabulous performance to secure a valuable point as City remained in 21st position. At the other end, Stoke goalkeeper, Steve Simonsen, saved Gary McSheffrey's penalty in front of the West Terrace.

SUNDAY 27TH FEBRUARY 1955

Initially released by the Sky Blues as a youngster, Kirk Stephens, born in Coventry on this day, joined Nuneaton Borough before Luton Town signed him in 1978. In the summer of 1984 he was signed by Bobby Gould for £50,000 and played 37 first-team games before a knee injury led to his premature retirement at the age of 31. His two goals for his hometown club came within three days of each other, both at Highfield Road in a loss to West Ham United and a 4-0 thrashing of Stoke City.

SATURDAY 27TH FEBRUARY 1999

Most Sky Blues supporters can remember where they were the day a league game was finally won at Villa Park. A crowd of 38,799 at the home of Aston Villa witnessed the 4-1 destruction by their local rivals. Just over a year on from the cup victory you began to wonder why it took so long to end the jinx. Doubles from John Aloisi and George Boateng sandwiched a penalty from Dion Dublin as City secured one of only three away victories in the season. The long wait of 63 years for a victory remains the only league win at Villa Park.

TUESDAY 28TH FEBRUARY 1928

Eddie Brown, who scored the quickest-ever league goal for Coventry, was born in Preston. Brown scored after just 12 seconds in a 2-2 draw with Southend United at Roots Hall in January 1954. He would go on to make 89 first-team appearances and scored 51 goals during his four seasons at Highfield Road.

FRIDAY 28TH FEBRUARY 1932

Noel Cantwell, who replaced Jimmy Hill as City manager at the beginning of their top flight era, was born in County Cork, Irish Free State. Cantwell played for West Ham United and captained Manchester United in the 1963 FA Cup Final before moving into management. He led the Sky Blues into their first-ever European campaign following a sixth-place finish in season 1969/70 before his sacking in March 1972. Cantwell sadly died on September 8th 2005, aged 73. His former teams held a minute's silence before their respective matches as a tribute.

THURSDAY 28th FEBRUARY 1974

Gordon Strachan was delighted when he signed Lee Carsley from Blackburn Rovers in December 2000. He told *BBC Sport:* "I made up my mind that I wanted Lee here early in the year when I knew that Gary McAllister was leaving. It has taken a long time and it has been down to perseverance." Born in Birmingham on this day, Carsley was equally delighted to be at Coventry: "I spoke to Gordon Strachan and was impressed with what he had to say. He said that we have got a fight on our hands but we are very confident." Carsley would be a leading light in City's subsequent relegation and moved back to the Premier League with Everton in February 2002 after 52 first-team appearances and six goals in sky blue.

SATURDAY 28th FEBRUARY 1998

A 3-0 victory at Crystal Palace saw the Sky Blues move up to tenth in the top division and established a new club record of seven straight wins. Palace would finish bottom with just two home wins all season. A rampant Coventry won with goals from Paul Telfer, Viorel Moldovan and Dion Dublin.

SATURDAY 29th FEBRUARY 1992

A rare leap year Saturday welcomed Manchester United to Highfield Road. Don Howe's City side maintained their 17th position in the Barclays League Division One by holding the eventual runners-up to a goalless draw in front of 23,962 fans. The Sky Blues' side comprised Steve Ogrizovic, Lloyd McGrath, Kenny Sansom, Stewart Robson, Andy Pearce, Peter Atherton, Sean Flynn, Dean Emerson, Robert Rosario, Kevin Gallacher and Paul Furlong.

FRIDAY 29th FEBRUARY 2008

The coming week would see Chris Coleman announce which players he would retain for the coming season. With 13 players out of contract there were big decisions to be taken; those included Stephen Hughes, Arjan De Zeeuw, Ellery Cairo and Marcus Hall. Coleman spoke to the *Coventry Evening Telegraph*: "We are going to be as honest as we can. Players are out of contract so it is not easy for them and some of the staff are nervous because they don't know whether they are going or staying."

COVENTRY CITY
On This Day

MARCH

SATURDAY 1st MARCH 1980

Nicky Phillips made his Coventry debut away to Brighton & Hove Albion in a 1-1 draw at the Goldstone Ground. His impressive start saw him play the next three matches in the number four shirt before going back to the reserves. He appeared as a substitute later in the season for Roger Van Gool in a 2-1 win over Crystal Palace but never played for the club again.

WEDNESDAY 2nd MARCH 1988

The Full Members Cup was created for the top two divisions after the exclusion from Europe in 1985. Coventry were within one game of a return to Wembley as Division Two Reading stood before a visit to the twin towers. The game ended 1-1 and went to penalties. Steve Sedgley and Dave Bennett missed their kicks as Michael Gilkes scored Reading's fifth to send them into the final where they defeated Luton Town 4-1.

SATURDAY 2nd MARCH 1991

Terry Butcher signed Ray Woods from Wigan Athletic for £200,000. A right winger, he made his debut in a 3-1 win over Crystal Palace and created the third goal for Brian Kilcline. Woods suffered with groin problems and made just 23 first-team appearances in 18 months. His solitary goal came against Peter Shilton in a 3-0 victory over relegated Derby County. He left City prior to the beginning of the Premier League but remembers his time well as he spoke to *Givemefootball.com*: "Physically and technically I coped quite well with the division but you had to be mentally stronger so you couldn't afford to switch off for a second. I played against teams like Liverpool and Arsenal and no-one can ever take away from me the fact that I played at the highest level in English football."

TUESDAY 2nd MARCH 2004

Coventry went down to ten men within the first minute after on-loan Peter Clarke lunged in two-footed on John Robinson. Scott Shearer saved Graham Kavanagh's first-half penalty before a Julian Joachim counter attack saw him upended by goalkeeper Martyn Margetson. The Cardiff custodian saw red before substitute goalkeeper Neil Alexander was beaten by Gary McSheffrey's 70th-minute penalty.

SATURDAY 3RD MARCH 2007

The 'Dowie' factor was still very much in evidence as a second successive home win ensured an unbeaten start for City's newly appointed manager. Goals from Michael Doyle and Leon McKenzie secured a 2-0 win over Hull City. A crowd of 21,079 witnessed a battling win over a Hull side who would finish one place off the relegation zone. Dowie was full of praise as he spoke to *The Independent*: "The squad have done brilliantly today. Credit must go to the lads. This is a good place to come and work. They have been working very hard but they are having fun too." Phil Brown, Hull City's manager, was less complimentary of his team: "It was a black and white performance. There were harsh words said at half-time but it wasn't to be."

SATURDAY 4TH MARCH 1933

By half-time Coventry City had raced into a 7-0 lead against Queens Park Rangers at Highfield Road. There were no further goals scored in the second half as Harry Storer's free-scoring side hit new heights. Billy Lake with a hat-trick led the rout as Clarrie Bourton chipped in with a brace.

FRIDAY 4TH MARCH 1966

Robert Rosario, who was signed by Terry Butcher for £650,000 from Norwich City, was born in Hammersmith. After his arrival in March 1991, injuries prevented him from making his full debut until the following August. For the majority of the season he partnered Kevin Gallacher but it was the arrival of Mick Quinn in November 1992 that triggered an upturn in Rosario's form. The famous eight-minute spell on Boxing Day destroyed Aston Villa as the stadium savoured a 3-0 victory inspired by the Rosario-Quinn partnership. Brian Clough made him his last-ever signing for Nottingham Forest in March 1993, paying £500,000.

SATURDAY 4TH MARCH 1978

England's World Cup-winning manager, Sir Alf Ramsey, managed Birmingham City between September 1977 and March 1978. His final game in English management was at Highfield Road as City won 4-0. Mick Ferguson scored a hat-trick and John Beck completed the scoring.

WEDNESDAY 5TH MARCH 2003

A dreadful performance at Hillsborough saw the Owls thrash City 5-1. Julian Joachim reduced the deficit to 2-1 but the scoreline was completed after just 69 minutes through goals from Michael Reddy, Shefki Kuqi (2), Paul McLaren and Lee Bradbury.

WEDNESDAY 6TH MARCH 1968

In the early hours, a major blaze destroyed the Main Stand at Highfield Road. Smoke billowed out of the stand roof, spotted shortly after 7am. Within minutes, fire engines were at the scene of devastation and houses in King Richard Street had to be evacuated. Damage escalated to the boardroom, directors' room, Viking Club, press box, sky blue shop, dressing rooms, commercial offices and many bars. Club records, photographs and the Second Division championship trophy all succumbed. Within hours it was announced that a new stand would be built as a priority. Season 1968/69 started only a week later than scheduled as the new £150,000 Main Stand was built in amazingly quick time.

SATURDAY 7TH MARCH 1987

Signed from Rotherham United in October 1986, Dean Emerson had starred in the two legged Littlewoods Cup tie just twelve days previously. John Sillett moved to sign central midfielder Emerson, a Stretford Ender as a youngster. On an icy, cold March day, Emerson went into a tackle with Gary Megson and damaged his knee. As well as missing out on Wembley, he did not return to the team until the 31st October after undergoing two operations. His appearances reflected his ongoing injury problems as he made 19, 18, 12, 20 and ten seasonal appearances before leaving the club for Hartlepool United as the Premier League began.

SATURDAY 7TH MARCH 1998

FA Cup quarter-final day saw Sheffield United visit Highfield Road for a place in the last four. A crowd of 23,084 saw Dion Dublin give City the lead only for Marcelo to level on half-time. The Blades were there for the taking and City missed out on a golden opportunity to get within 90 minutes of a return to Wembley. Sheffield United won the replay on penalties then lost to Newcastle United at Old Trafford in the semi-final.

THURSDAY 8TH MARCH 2007

Talking to *Sky Sports News*, Iain Dowie spoke about the proposed takeover by the Manhattan Group: "The club is in good hands in terms of the senior management team and they will make the right decisions for Coventry. I think if you listened to Geoffrey Robinson's statement he said exactly that. He said he hopes it happens but it's whether the deal is right. Far more eloquent financial people are dealing with that side of things now and I am a very interested bystander."

FRIDAY 9TH MARCH 1973

Steve Froggatt, who joined Coventry for £1.9 million in October 1998, was born in Lincoln. His debut came against former club Aston Villa and saw the claret and blues win 2-1 at Highfield Road. In February 2000, Froggatt was injured in a tackle by Nicky Summerbee that would eventually end his career at the age of just 28. After retiring in the summer of 2001, Froggatt worked as the press officer at City before setting up his own personal fitness training company. In total he played 56 times for the club, scoring four times.

SATURDAY 9TH MARCH 1985

Don Mackay replaced Bobby Gould as manager after an initial caretaker spell of nine matches which brought four victories, one of those from a Terry Gibson winner at Old Trafford. Previously assistant manager under Gould's tenure, Mackay's first game in full charge saw the Sky Blues defeat Queens Park Rangers 3-0 at Highfield Road. With Stuart Pearce captaining the side, Terry Gibson (two) and a Brian Kilcline header took the Sky Blues up to 17th in Division One.

MONDAY 10TH MARCH 1919

The club's application to join the Football League was successful, having canvassed 25 votes. Highfield Road averaged gates of 8,000 although its capacity was now three times that amount. Christmas Day saw the Sky Blues record their first win, a 3-2 victory at home to Stoke City, and immediate relegation was avoided with five points from the last three matches (two points for a win back then).

THURSDAY 10TH MARCH 1938

Mick Kearns, who made 385 first-team appearances and scored 16 goals for his only club, was born in Nuneaton. He made his debut at home to Bournemouth in September 1957 and up until his retirement in the summer of 1968 played in five different divisions. Alongside George Curtis and Ron Farmer, he helped City climb out of Division Three and won two promotions in four seasons.

TUESDAY 10TH MARCH 1964

Signed from Heart of Midlothian by Bobby Gould for £160,000 in December 1984, David Bowman wore the number four shirt in central midfield. Born on this day in Tunbridge Wells, he made 48 first-team appearances and scored three goals in his two seasons. His career ended at Forfar Athletic where he made headlines for his sending off against Berwick Rangers. Originally sent off for two cautions, Bowman was reported for using foul and abusive language on three separate occasions which totalled four red cards. He received a seven-match ban for his troubles.

SATURDAY 10TH MARCH 1973

Maine Road witnessed its first-ever Coventry City victory with goals from Willie Carr and Colin Stein. Joint manager, Joe Mercer, returned to Manchester City for the first time since his departure the previous season. A crowd of 30,448 saw the Sky Blues move up to tenth but they would finish the season in 19th after seven straight defeats up to season end. Tommy Booth scored Manchester City's equaliser while Francis Lee's penalty kick was saved by Bill Glazier.

SATURDAY 11TH MARCH 1972

Noel Cantwell's final match in charge of Coventry City saw a 1-0 defeat at Elland Road to runners-up elect, Leeds United. Jack Charlton scored the winning goal for Leeds who would remain unbeaten all season at home. Cantwell crafted the club's highest-ever top-division placing of sixth and took the Sky Blues into Europe for the first time. Chief scout, Bob Dennison, took over until the end of the season upon when Joe Mercer and Gordon Milne were appointed joint managers.

WEDNESDAY 12TH MARCH 2008

An unexploded World War II Luftwaffe bomb was discovered on a building site near the old Highfield Road site in Coventry town centre. An army bomb disposal unit was called in with a controlled explosion carried out nearly 15 hours later at 2.40am.

WEDNESDAY 13TH MARCH 1968

Signed at the age of 23 from Halesowen Town, Sean Flynn scored on his Sky Blues debut at Bramall Lane in a 3-0 Boxing Day thumping of Sheffield United. His cross shot from the right-hand edge of the penalty area soared into the top corner of the net in front of the travelling hordes. Born in Birmingham on this day, Flynn played 105 times and scored ten goals between December 1991 and his departure to Derby County in the summer of 1995.

WEDNESDAY 13TH MARCH 1991

Signed at the age of 24 for £15,000, again from Halesowen Town, by Terry Butcher, Andy Pearce scored the winning goal on his home debut. The 2-1 victory over Luton Town was sealed by his diving header with seven minutes remaining. A replacement for cup-winning captain, Brian Kilcline, Pearce made 81 appearances between March 1991 and his departure to Sheffield Wednesday for £500,000 in 1993. He scored four goals yet is famously remembered by Sky Blues' supporters for his own goal at Loftus Road in February 1993. His attempted clearance spun off his boot and into the net from just outside his own penalty area leaving Steve Ogrizovic stranded.

SATURDAY 14TH MARCH 1987

Around 15,000 Sky Blues supporters made their way to Hillsborough for the FA Cup quarter-final tie. Sheffield Wednesday boasted an impressive unbeaten home run in the trophy dating back 23 matches and 48,005 were present to watch City, resplendent in their all-yellow away kit, turn the form book on its head. Cyrille Regis opened the scoring before Gary Megson equalised with the first goal conceded by the Sky Blues during the cup run. Enter Keith Houchen with 78th- and 83rd-minute breakaway goals to send Coventry into the FA Cup semi-finals for the first time in their history.

TUESDAY 14TH MARCH 1995

Peter Ndlovu became the first visiting player for 33 years to score a hat-trick in a league game at Anfield. City's 3-2 victory took them up to ninth in the Premier League and Liverpool would concede just 13 goals at home all season. Former Liverpool players David Burrows and Mike Marsh lined up for Coventry who would end the season with a slide down to 16th. Only 27,183 attended the match, a surprising statistic with Liverpool having reached the Coca Cola Cup final and on a long unbeaten run.

SATURDAY 15TH MARCH 1930

Norwich City recorded their biggest-ever victory, a 10-2 win over Coventry City. Prior to Carrow Road, the game was played at The Nest and only 8,230 supporters witnessed Tommy Hunt's five-goal performance. The scoreline in the Division Three (South) match remains the Sky Blues' record league defeat.

SATURDAY 15TH MARCH 1997

A 4-0 defeat at St. James'Park saw the Sky Blues drop to 16th position in the table. Goals from Steve Watson, Robert Lee, Peter Beardsley and Robbie Elliott for the eventual Premier League runners-up destroyed Coventry. Brian Borrows' late sending off gave him the unenviable statistic of being the first-ever Coventry substitute to be sent off in the club's history.

SATURDAY 16TH MARCH 1968

The second highest ever attendance at Highfield Road, 47,111, watched the Sky Blues beat Manchester United 2-0. Goals from Ernie Machin and Maurice Setters defeated the European champions in Coventry's first season in Division One.

WEDNESDAY 17TH MARCH 1943

Ernie Hunt, who joined the Sky Blues from Everton in March 1968 for £65,000, was born in Swindon. Hunt would go on to play 173 first-team games and scored 51 goals during his five seasons with the club. Along with Willie Carr he became famous for the brilliant implementation of the 'donkey kick'. Carr's back-heeled flick up for Hunt to volley into the back of Everton's net in October 1970 would be shown on countless occasions on *Match of the Day*.

SATURDAY 17TH MARCH 1990

Dave Bennett became the first member of Coventry City's FA Cup-winning side to return to Highfield Road with his new club. Coming on as substitute for David Hirst, all four sides of the stadium stood to welcome him with warm applause. Sheffield Wednesday led 4-1 by the time 'Benno' entered the pitch yet this did not stop the faithful from showing their appreciation of his efforts in sky blue. He currently resides at the Ricoh on Saturday afternoons as part of the Mercia team providing match analysis and commentary.

TUESDAY 17TH MARCH 1998

A crowd of 29,034 witnessed a superb FA Cup quarter-final replay at Bramall Lane. The Sky Blues led through Paul Telfer's tenth-minute long-range free kick. Brother of future Sky Blue Dean, David Holdsworth, squeezed in an equaliser with 89 minutes on the clock. Extra time came and went and so it was on to the first penalty shoot-out since the defeat at Reading in the Simod Cup. Missed penalties by Dion Dublin, Simon Haworth and David Burrows saw the Blades win 3-1 and book a semi-final with Newcastle United.

SATURDAY 18TH MARCH 1961

Coventry number one Arthur Lightening was replaced by Bob Wesson after injury following the 2-1 home defeat to Walsall. Signed along with Ron Farmer from Nottingham Forest, Lightening made 165 first-team appearances before Jimmy Hill sold him to Middlesbrough in September 1962. Bob Wesson replaced Lightening and made 156 first-team appearances between 1961 and 1964 before Bill Glazier joined the Sky Blues. Glazier would remain the undisputed number one for ten seasons.

SATURDAY 18TH MARCH 1967

Coventry's long unbeaten run captured the nation's imagination as they featured on *Match of the Day* for the first time in the Division Two clash with Bolton Wanderers at Highfield Road. Bobby Gould's goal ensured City took a point from the game as they continued their push for the top flight. The 28,850 supporters were able to watch it all over again from the comfort of their armchairs later on that evening.

THURSDAY 19TH MARCH 1964

Signed by Bobby Gould from Blackburn Rovers in April 1993, Roy Wegerle made 63 first-team appearances and scored 11 goals. Born in Pretoria, South Africa on this day, Wegerle starred in the 'hole' just behind Mick Quinn and Peter Ndlovu as the Sky Blues began season 1993/94 with an eight-game unbeaten run. In the summer of 1995 he was released and went to the USA to join the inauguration of the Major League Soccer (MLS).

MONDAY 19TH MARCH 1973

Magnus Hedman, who was the club's most capped individual during his stay with the club, was born in Huddinge, Sweden. He appeared 38 times for Sweden during his five years at Coventry. Hedman joined from AIK Stockholm in July 1997 as heir apparent to Steve Ogrizovic and departed for Celtic in the summer of 2002 after 151 first-team appearances.

TUESDAY 19TH MARCH 1979

In a season where the side finished in tenth position with an excellent home record, it was hard to believe the campaign would include a 7-1 defeat at West Bromwich Albion, a 5-0 defeat at Bristol City and a 5-1 thrashing by Queens Park Rangers. All of the above were on their travels and included trebles for Joe Royle (Bristol City) and Clive Allen (QPR) with a double for Cyrille Regis (WBA). A total of 29 of City's 44 points were collected at fortress Highfield Road and two of those were in a fantastic 4-3 win over Manchester United under the floodlights. Goals from Barry Powell, Garry Thompson, Tommy Hutchison and Bobby McDonald gave the Sky Blues a 4-1 lead after 51 minutes. Sammy McIlroy and a second for Steve Coppell made the scoreline slightly better reading for United supporters in the following morning's newspapers.

SATURDAY 20TH MARCH 1999

On loan Venezia striker Stefano Gioacchini made just three substitute appearances for Coventry during his brief stay at the club. His debut came at Highbury on the same day Lee Dixon made his 500th appearance for Arsenal. Gordon Strachan named Gioacchini on the bench and introduced him for Trond Soldvedt after 77 minutes. He returned to Italy at the end of the season and signed for Salernitana.

SATURDAY 21st MARCH 1992

The first-ever Ladies' Day at Highfield Road welcomed Oldham Athletic as the visitors and a crowd of 13,042. To gauge the success of the experiment, the following home game against Arsenal attracted 14,119. Bearing in mind the Gunners' away support is much stronger than Oldham Athletic, it seemed apparent that not many ladies returned. Andy Pearce's opening goal was cancelled out by Nick Henry and the points were shared.

FRIDAY 21st MARCH 2008

Richard Duffy joined Coventry on loan for a record fourth time. The right-back was signed initially by Micky Adams in February 2005 and made 15 first-team appearances. Adams then signed him on a season-long loan in August 2005 and Duffy made 34 appearances before returning to his parent club, Portsmouth. In October 2006 he was signed, by Adams, for a third time to cover for an injury to Andy Whing and played 13 first-team games. Chris Coleman signed his fellow Welshman to enable stop-gap full-back Isaac Osbourne to return to his more familiar central midfield berth. The plan backfired, however, when Duffy picked up an injury and was ruled out for the season after just two appearances. In total he played 64 times for Coventry and did not score a single goal.

SATURDAY 22nd MARCH 1969

The Sky Blues handed out a 4-1 defeat to Burnley at Highfield Road. Goalless at half-time, Dave Clements, Neil Martin, Ernie Hunt and Ernie Machin kept Coventry in 20th position, one above the relegation zone and where they would finish the season.

FRIDAY 22nd MARCH 2002

Fulham midfielder Paul Trollope joined the Sky Blues on a deal until the end of the season. Signed on the same day as Horacio Carbonari, Trollope went straight into the team on the left side of midfield for the forthcoming derby with fellow play-off chasers Birmingham City. He made just six first-team appearances before he was released in the summer of 2002 upon the arrival of Gary McAllister as manager.

SATURDAY 23RD MARCH 1968

City's first top flight visit to Roker Park saw them leave with a point thanks to Ernie Hunt's equaliser after Malcolm Hunt scored on his debut for the Mackems. A crowd of 26,286 watched Sunderland start their recovery which would ensure their top-flight survival come May.

WEDNESDAY 24TH MARCH 1976

Recently released by former manager Chris Coleman, Marcus Hall was born in Coventry. He made his 300th first-team appearance for the club in the 2-2 draw at home to Watford in the final game of season 2008/09. Uniquely in football nowadays, he has never transferred between clubs for any fee. His debut came as substitute in a 4-0 home defeat to Tottenham Hotspur in 1994, as he replaced Paul Cook. After moving to Southampton, Nottingham Forest and Stoke City, he was re-signed by Micky Adams in 2005. His two first-team goals came within two months of each other and, predominantly left-footed, his debut goal was a right-foot screamer against Everton at Highfield Road in the Coca Cola Cup in October 1997.

SATURDAY 24TH MARCH 1984

Signed from Bristol Rovers for £5,000 in the summer of 1983, Graham Withey scored on his debut at White Hart Lane as substitute for Martin Singleton. In the reverse fixture, Tottenham destroyed the Sky Blues 4-2 as goals from Withey, and a penalty from Gerry Daly, were mere consolations. Withey stayed for 18 months at Highfield Road and made 27 first-team appearances, scoring seven goals, before transferring to Cardiff City.

TUESDAY 24TH MARCH 1987

Wimbledon would remain in the top division for 14 seasons. City first visited Plough Lane three weeks before the FA Cup semi-final against Leeds United at Hillsborough. Just 4,370 watched the game as the 'Crazy Gang' won 2-1 with goals from John Fashanu and Carlton Fairweather. Michael Gynn had given the Sky Blues an early lead and City remained in eighth position. Wimbledon would finish their first top-flight season in sixth and, managed by former City manager Bobby Gould, would go on to defeat Liverpool at Wembley in the FA Cup Final the following May.

MONDAY 25TH MARCH 1996

Sky sent their *Monday Night Football* show to The Dell for an 18th versus 17th showdown with just eight games remaining. Jason Dodd's goal after just two minutes won the game for Southampton as the Sky Blues extended their winless run to five games. The real fireworks occurred in the tunnel after the game as Sky's Andy Gray and Richard Keys went live to Ron Atkinson. Gray commented that City were in trouble and seemed to lack commitment to the cause. Atkinson retorted: "I'm sorry, you can sit there and play with all your silly machines, if the boys play badly I'll whip 'em, but I ain't whipping them for that. Who was man-of-the-match by the way?" Richard Keys advised it was Saints goalkeeper Dave Beasant which only infuriated Ron more: "So we must have played not bad then. Thanks lads, goodnight."

TUESDAY 26TH MARCH 1963

Division Three Coventry City took the 'giant-killer' tag with a superb 2-1 win over Division Two Sunderland at Highfield Road. Trailing to John Crossan's 33rd-minute goal in this FA Cup fifth-round tie, City equalised through Dietmar Bruck with eight minutes remaining. Just three minutes later, right-back John Sillett floated a free kick into Sunderland's penalty area from where George Curtis powered a header past Jim Montgomery to send City to a quarter-final with Manchester United.

FRIDAY 26TH MARCH 2010

Express delivery company, City Link, signed a three-year deal to become official sponsors from the start of season 2010/11. The deal was the biggest-ever for the Sky Blues and replaced property development firm Cassidy Developments who sponsored the club for the previous five years. Commercial director, Nathan Kosky, speaking to the official club website said: "This is very good news for all parties. We are taking our relationship with City Link to a new level and its support will be a key part of the club's development over the next few years and hopefully beyond. At the same time, we are sure our growing profile nationally and internationally will help City Link achieve its own business goals."

MONDAY 27TH MARCH 1950

Signed by Gordon Milne from all-conquering Leeds United in the summer of 1976, Terry Yorath was born in Cardiff. A Welsh international captain, Yorath patrolled central midfield and made 107 first-team appearances, scoring three goals. He made his debut in a 3-1 home defeat to reigning champions Liverpool and bowed out of Highfield Road injured in a 3-2 victory over Bristol City in April 1979. In October 1978 captain Yorath, resplendent in the new brown away kit, led the Sky Blues out at The Hawthorns. They returned to the dressing room 90 minutes later on the end of a 7-1 thrashing. He moved to Tottenham Hotspur for £275,000 before moving into league management before becoming the Wales national team manager in 1988.

SATURDAY 27TH MARCH 1971

A colour clash with Huddersfield Town's blue and white stripes ensured the Sky Blues took to the field in yellow shirts borrowed from their hosts. A crowd of 15,141 packed into Leeds Road as Huddersfield collected another two points with a 1-0 win.

WEDNESDAY 28TH MARCH 1973

Highfield Road was chosen to host the Northern Ireland versus Portugal World Cup qualifier. The group six match drew an attendance of only 11,273 who witnessed a Martin O'Neill goal equalised by Eusebio who slotted a penalty past Pat Jennings with just six minutes remaining. Former Sky Blue Dave Clements lined up for Northern Ireland but the game gave the City public the opportunity to watch the great Eusebio live in action before his retirement in 1978.

SUNDAY 29TH MARCH 1970

Alan Miller, who played just one competitive match for Coventry, was born in Epping. Signed on loan as cover for Chris Kirkland, he was called into action in the 24th minute after Kirkland was sent off for a foul on Jimmy Floyd Hasselbaink. The 66 minutes he spent on the pitch at Stamford Bridge saw him pick the ball out of his net six times as the Sky Blues surrendered 6-1. Miller never played another first-team game for City and retired from professional football with a back injury in 1993.

TUESDAY 30TH MARCH 1943

Signed by Jimmy Hill from Middlesbrough for a then club record transfer fee of £57,500, Ian Gibson made 104 first-team appearances for the Sky Blues. Born in Newton Stewart, Scotland, Gibson scored 15 goals for Coventry between 1966 and the summer of 1970 when he was sold to Division Two Cardiff City for £35,000. The Sky Blues' unbeaten run of 25 games in season 1966/67 would see them clinch promotion to Division One and Gibson's midfield form was seen as one of the major factors in the club's success that season. He retired from football in 1974 with injuries that had plagued him throughout his career finally catching up with him.

SATURDAY 31ST MARCH 1984

After 32 minutes Dave Bennett opened the scoring for the Sky Blues against Arsenal at Highfield Road. Just seven minutes later, Chris Whyte, later to play just one first-team game for Coventry (season 1995/96 in a 5-0 win over Blackburn Rovers played with an orange ball) equalised for the Gunners. Somehow, Arsenal ran out 4-1 winners, down to ten men and with a central midfielder in goal for the last half hour. Pat Jennings went off injured and was replaced in goal by former Sky Blues Player of the Year (91/92) Stewart Robson who had just scored to make it 2-1. Whyte then received a red card for retaliation before Arsenal added further agony with goals from Brian Talbot and Paul Mariner. Only 10,533 witnessed the drama as City dropped a place to 17th.

SATURDAY 31ST MARCH 2001

One of only four home wins in a rotten season, the Sky Blues defeated Derby County 2-0 to maintain the 19th position the side had remained in since the middle of January. This was one of the better performances as goals from Moustapha Hadji and John Hartson either side of half-time gave hope to City supporters that relegation could be avoided. The last victory had come on Boxing Day at Everton with Hartson's late season arrival the catalyst for the improvement that would end in tears. Former Coventry assistant manager Jim Smith managed Derby for a number of their Premier League years while future loan signing Horacio Carbonari lined up in the centre of Derby's defence.

COVENTRY CITY
On This Day

APRIL

SATURDAY 1st APRIL 1967

Signed by John Sillett and George Curtis from Wolverhampton Wanderers, Graham Rodger, who was born in Glasgow, made his debut at Highfield Road in a 3-0 defeat to eventual champions, Liverpool, in November 1985. Rodger shot to prominence when he replaced Brian Kilcline before the end of normal time at Wembley in the FA Cup final. In the first period of extra time his left foot sent the ball over to the right wing where Lloyd McGrath was waiting, away from the attentions of Glenn Hoddle. We all know what happened next. A central defender, Rodger made 43 first-team appearances and scored two goals, before he moved to Luton Town in the summer of 1989.

SATURDAY 1st APRIL 2000

Steve Ogrizovic made his 600th first-team appearance against one of his former clubs. The largest crowd of the season at Highfield Road, 23,084, witnessed a 2-0 half-time lead for the once mighty Reds. Michael Owen ended the game as a contest before Emile Heskey made it 3-0 with 12 minutes remaining.

TUESDAY 1st APRIL 2008

Having lingered no higher than 18th position since the turn of 2008, loan signing Zavon Hines' late goal looked to have given the Sky Blues a most valuable three points in their bid to climb away from the drop zone. Sheffield Wednesday had suffered a postponement and abandonment in this fixture back in February as Chris Coleman was appointed Sky Blues' manager. Richard Wood, highly sought after by Coleman, headed an equaliser two minutes into added time to prolong the nerves of City followers.

SATURDAY 2nd APRIL 1977

The Sky Blues' 1-1 draw with Tottenham Hotspur at Highfield Road was the first home fixture since a similar scoreline with Middlesbrough on the 22nd January. The winter weather during this spell brought a spate of postponements and ensured three straight home games to finish the season, such was the backlog. Coventry were in 17th position at the start of April having played seven consecutive away games of which they won only one, at Elland Road of all places.

TUESDAY 3RD APRIL 1979

Arsenal left-back Sammy Nelson incurred the wrath of the Football Association with his equalising goal celebration against the Sky Blues at Highbury. Arsenal suspended him for two weeks and he was fined a fortnight's wages after he 'mooned' to the North Bank having levelled the score with 14 minutes remaining. Steve Hunt had given Coventry the lead in the first half before Nelson strode up from full-back to smash home past Les Sealey.

TUESDAY 4TH APRIL 1944

Born in Ystradgynlais, South Wales on this day, Ronnie Rees made his debut as an 18-year-old in September 1962 under Jimmy Hill. Rees featured in two promotions over the next six seasons as the Sky Blues reached the top flight. He played for Wales on 39 occasions and scored 52 goals in 262 first-team appearances before he was sold by Noel Cantwell to West Bromwich Albion for £65,000.

SATURDAY 5TH APRIL 1952

Dennis Mortimer, who was born in Liverpool, made his City debut as substitute in a 2-2 draw with West Ham United at Highfield Road in 1969. After 222 first-team appearances and 12 goals, Mortimer's midfield composure and ball skills were sold up the A45 to local rivals Aston Villa. Mortimer would go on to lead Villa to league title and European Cup success in over 300 appearances for the claret and blues.

SATURDAY 5TH APRIL 1975

John Hartson was born on this day. Although he only made 12 first-team appearances for Coventry City, the six goals he scored almost single-handedly kept the Sky Blues in the Premier League. Hartson's strength and heading ability were vital to prolonging the season to the penultimate game at Villa Park.

SATURDAY 5TH APRIL 1975

Carlisle United spent just one season in the top division. After three games of season 1974/75 they were top of the league having defeated Chelsea at Stamford Bridge. By April, their fate was sealed in a goalless draw at Highfield Road as they bowed out with four matches remaining.

MONDAY 6TH APRIL 1970

Born in Wigan on this day, Peter Atherton was signed by Terry Butcher as a straight replacement for Trevor Peake. Atherton played 120 first-team games in three consistent seasons and failed to find the net. His centre-half partners included Andy Pearce and Peter Billing before a steady final season alongside Phil Babb, prior to his move to Liverpool. Sheffield Wednesday signed him for £800,000 before he moved on to Bradford City where he ended his career.

SATURDAY 7TH APRIL 1984

Tommy Langley's second and final on-loan appearance for the Sky Blues came at Villa Park in a 2-0 defeat. Goals from Brendan Ormsby and the late Paul Birch kept Coventry in 17th position and ensured that new strike power was needed. Langley had enjoyed success with Chelsea, Queens Park Rangers and Crystal Palace prior to joining City on loan from AEK Athens. Aged 32, his best days were behind him and City turned to Mick Ferguson to secure their survival with three goals in seven games.

WEDNESDAY 8TH APRIL 1931

Harry Storer was appointed Coventry City manager by chairman Walter Brandish as the club looked to move out of Division Three (South). Dick Bayliss was appointed as chief scout and the two of them would bring the likes of Clarrie Bourton and Jock Lauderdale to the club. The 1930s provided huge entertainment for City supporters with over 100 goals scored in seasons 1931/32, 1932/33 and 1933/34. This led to promotion to Division Two in May 1936 where they would remain until relegation in 1952.

SATURDAY 8TH APRIL 1989

Norwich City, throughout season 1988/89, remained in the top six of Division One. Their title challenge fell apart as the Sky Blues came from a goal down to win 2-1 thanks to David Phillips and David Speedie. Goalkeeper Bryan Gunn was sent off in added time which led to Mark Bowen taking the jersey to face a Brian Kilcline penalty. Following misses against Everton, Wimbledon and Arsenal (all at Highfield Road), 'Killer' missed his fourth of the season as he dragged his shot wide.

MONDAY 8TH APRIL 1996

David Busst joined Coventry from non-league Moor Green in 1991 aged 24. His 60th and final first-team appearance came on this day at Old Trafford when he was sadly injured in a collision with Denis Irwin and Brian McClair. A week prior he had starred in a 1-0 win over Liverpool at Highfield Road in front of 23,037. The Old Trafford faithful, all 50,322 of them, afforded him a standing ovation as he was stretchered off the pitch for the final time as a Coventry player.

SATURDAY 9TH APRIL 1977

A knee injury to Jim Blyth saw the City goalkeeper stretchered off with 30 minutes remaining at home to West Ham United. With no substitute goalkeepers, left-back Bobby McDonald took over in goal and watched Mick Ferguson head City into the lead with 15 minutes remaining. It was not to be a fairytale ending as Bryan 'Pop' Robson levelled with just five minutes on the clock. Blyth would be ruled out for the season and Les Sealey would make his first-team debut two days later against Queens Park Rangers.

WEDNESDAY 9TH APRIL 1997

The visit of Ruud Gullit's Chelsea was delayed by 15 minutes due to 'technical problems'. Chelsea's kit man packed only the Londoners' blue home kit which clashed with City's sky blue/dark blue stripes. They took to the pitch resplendent in the Sky Blues' chess board style away kit of red and blue and faced a City side which included 40-year-old Gordon Strachan. Three second-half goals in eleven minutes from Dion Dublin, Paul Williams and Noel Whelan gave City a 3-1 win.

SATURDAY 10TH APRIL 2004

Signed on loan from Rushden & Diamonds by Eric Black, Onandi Lowe made his debut as substitute in a 4-0 thrashing of Millwall at Highfield Road. His second and only full appearance two days later saw him score the consolation goal in a disappointing 3-1 defeat at Crewe Alexandra. Personal circumstances ensured that he was never seen again in a Coventry shirt and as soon as he had arrived Lowe was on his way out of the club.

TUESDAY 11TH APRIL 1961

City turned in a horror show at Vicarage Road as Watford won 7-2 in the Division Three match. A crowd of 10,514 watched Brian and Peter Hill offer nothing more than consolation goals as Billy Frith's men suffered their worst defeat since February 1958 when Southampton won 7-1 at The Dell.

SATURDAY 12TH APRIL 1986

Liverpool's 5-0 win over the Sky Blues at Anfield saw manager Don Mackay tender his resignation after the game. Having taken over from Bobby Gould at Christmas 1984 he left the club in a similar position to when he arrived – fighting relegation.

SUNDAY 12TH APRIL 1987

A return to Hillsborough for 27,000 City supporters as the club took on Leeds United in their first-ever FA Cup semi-final. A huge crowd of 51,372 were packed into the stadium to see Leeds take an early lead through future Sky Blue David Rennie. An inspired piece of play by Dave Bennett set up Michael Gynn for the equaliser before Keith Houchen's scrambled effort left the Sky Blues just 12 minutes from Wembley for the first time. Keith Edwards' header took the tie into extra time before Dave Bennett sent the fans delirious with the winner.

FRIDAY 12TH APRIL 2002

Roland Nilsson's last game in charge as Coventry manager saw Millwall boost their play-off chances with a 1-0 win at Highfield Road. Steve Claridge scored the only goal as City slumped to 11th having looked likely to secure a play-off berth themselves just two months earlier. Six defeats in the final seven games saw Nilsson leave the club.

SATURDAY 12TH APRIL 2003

At just 16 years and 167 days old, Ben Mackey became the youngest-ever player when he came on as substitute against Ipswich Town. On as a replacement for Jay Bothroyd, Mackey could do little to reverse the 4-2 scoreline as the Tractor Boys came from two goals down to score four times in just 17 minutes. Mackey made three substitute appearances for the Sky Blues before being released and moved into non-league football.

TUESDAY 13TH APRIL 1982

Martin Singleton made 28 first-team appearances for Coventry and scored twice during his stay at the club. He made his debut aged just 18 on this day against Everton at Highfield Road wearing the number eight shirt. With 36 minutes played he smashed the winner from the edge of the penalty area past Neville Southall's dive. Singleton joined Coventry as an apprentice before transferring to Bradford City in 1984. He was present at Valley Parade on the day of the tragic fire when 56 people died. Alongside him that day were former Sky Blues Terry Yorath, Eric McManus, John Hendrie and Greg Abbott.

SATURDAY 14TH APRIL 1956

Reg Matthews became the first Coventry City player to win a full England cap. He appeared alongside Tom Finney, Billy Wright, Nat Lofthouse and Duncan Edwards in a 1-1 draw at Hampden Park against Scotland. Matthews became the first player outside the top two divisions to become an England international as the Sky Blues were then in Division Three (South).

SUNDAY 14TH APRIL 1975

Andy Marshall, born in Bury St. Edmunds on this day, succeeded a plethora of goalkeeping signings when he joined in time for the start of season 2006/07. Marton Fulop, Stephen Bywater, Luke Steele, Ian Bennett, Scott Shearer, Gavin Ward, Fabien Debec and Morten Hyldgaard had all followed in Magnus Hedman's footsteps as City's number one. Marshall displayed fine form and supporters awarded him three Player of the Year trophies at the end of his first season. He made 68 first-team appearances, before the arrival of Keiren Westwood, and moved to Aston Villa when his contract expired in the summer of 2009.

SATURDAY 15TH APRIL 1989

The tragic events at Hillsborough put everything into perspective today. 96 Liverpool supporters died in a human crush and saw the FA Cup semi-final against Nottingham Forest abandoned after six minutes. While events were unfolding in Sheffield, the Sky Blues drew 2-2 at Kenilworth Road. Luton led twice and City replied with goals from Cyrille Regis and David Smith to earn a point.

SATURDAY 16TH APRIL 1983

With two minutes still to play, Coventry and Birmingham City remained goalless at Highfield Road. Enter the visitors' number six, midfielder Les Phillips. His goal sent their fans delirious and prompted a Coventry fan to run onto the pitch from the West Terrace, take off his replica shirt and slam it into the turf. In front of the directors' box his gesture saw him arrested yet receive a huge ovation from the similarly frustrated Coventry faithful.

FRIDAY 17TH APRIL 1981

Signed by Micky Adams in January 2007, Michael Mifsud was born in Pieta, Malta. Mifsud joined the Sky Blues on a two-and-a-half year deal and scored his first goal with a stunning volley at Plymouth Argyle in a 3-2 defeat. Prior to his release in June 2009, he played 95 first-team games and scored 23 goals. His stock hit major heights in September 2008 as 74,055 packed into Old Trafford to see him score both goals as City knocked the Premier League champions out of the Carling Cup.

SATURDAY 17TH APRIL 1993

Coventry's first Premier League visit to Anfield ended in a 4-0 defeat. Mark Walters' hat-trick and David Burrows' piledriver in front of 33,328 fans took Liverpool up to eighth and dropped the Sky Blues down to 12th position. Future Sky Blues Burrows and Don Hutchison starred for the home side still smarting from the 5-1 drubbing in the reverse game back in December.

TUESDAY 18TH APRIL 1972

Coventry moved away from the relegation zone with a hard fought 3-2 win over Sheffield United at Highfield Road. Luck was on the Sky Blues' side as the original game had been abandoned due to a snowstorm as the Yorkshire side led 2-0. Goals from Bobby Graham, Willie Carr and Ernie Machin gave City a 3-1 interval lead. The mercurial Tony Currie scored both for the Blades and narrowly missed out on a hat-trick. With Currie and Salmons in the United side, their line-up had a culinary feel to it. The introduction of Alan Woodward failed to find the equaliser.

SATURDAY 19TH APRIL 1952

Champions elect Sheffield Wednesday defeated the Sky Blues 2-0 at Highfield Road. The result relegated Coventry from Division Two into Division Three (South). Having lost 22 out of 42 league games, the outcome was never really in doubt. A total of 14 wins all season was not enough to extend the 16-season spell in Division Two and results would get worse before times would improve for City supporters.

SATURDAY 19TH APRIL 1986

John Sillett and George Curtis stepped up from their roles as executive director and youth team coach to lead the Sky Blues against Luton Town at Highfield Road. In their first game in charge we saw a revitalised Coventry City step onto the field of play. Nick Pickering's early second-half strike would have caught the corporates still indulging as he fired past Les Sealey.

MONDAY 20TH APRIL 1964

London Road, home of Peterborough United, set a new attendance record as the Sky Blue Army invaded. City were backed by 12,000 supporters who made the relatively short journey with many arriving late due to the dense traffic. A crowd of 26,307 watched the hosts win 2-0 and ensured a five-day wait for City's promotion to Division Two. The match was a 7.30pm kick off which meant rush hour and more for Sky Blues' followers. It would all be worth it when Colchester visited the following Saturday.

MONDAY 20TH APRIL 1987

With the FA Cup Final just 26 days away, a 4-1 win over Queens Park Rangers brought the 'Mexican Wave' to Highfield Road for the first time. Goals from Michael Gynn, Cyrille Regis (two) and a thumping volley from David Phillips ensured former Sky Blue Gary Bannister's strike was scant consolation.

SATURDAY 21ST APRIL 1979

City moved up to eighth in Division One with a 4-0 win over Southampton, inspired by a hat-trick from Ian Wallace. A crowd of 17,707 witnessed City's highly impressive home record maintained with Andy Blair completing the scoring.

TUESDAY 22ND APRIL 1969

On the day City held runners-up Liverpool to the goalless draw that ensured their survival, Dion Dublin was born in Leicester. Signed by Ron Atkinson for £2 million from Manchester United in September 1994, Dublin scored on his debut at Queens Park Rangers and went on to score in seven of his next nine matches. A total of 171 first-team appearances brought 72 goals and international recognition. Season 1997/98 brought 18 league goals as he topped the scoring chart with Michael Owen. To this day, Dublin remains Coventry's leading goalscorer in the top division.

TUESDAY 22ND APRIL 1969

Coventry stayed in Division One courtesy of Leicester City's inability to secure another two points. Leicester's season overlapped so City relied on others to secure their Division One status for a second successive year. Just one point separated the Sky Blues from their M69 rivals as they joined Queens Park Rangers in Division Two.

SATURDAY 22ND APRIL 1978

Having been promoted just the previous May from Division Two, Nottingham Forest took the title with a goalless draw at Highfield Road. Peter Shilton's fabulous save from Mick Ferguson's point-blank header ensured Forest took top spot with two games of the season remaining.

TUESDAY 23RD APRIL 1957

On the day City beat Bournemouth 4-2 at Highfield Road with a hat-trick from Ken McPherson in Division Three (South), Richard Keys was born in Coventry. The anchorman of Sky Sports live football coverage since its inception in August 1992, Keys is well known in the world of football for his support of the Sky Blues.

FRIDAY 23RD APRIL 1976

Born in Nottingham on this day, Darren Huckerby joined the Sky Blues from Newcastle United in November 1996 for £1 million. He left for Leeds United in August 1999 having played 109 first team games and scoring 34 goals. Season 1997/98 dovetailed him perfectly with Dion Dublin. Huckerby scored 14 Premier League goals while Dublin was joint league top scorer with 18.

SATURDAY 23RD APRIL 1983

Soon to be a Seagull, Steve Jacobs, was sent off at the Goldstone Ground after a brawl with full-back Chris Ramsey. Just six days after Brighton secured an FA Cup Final place there was a carnival atmosphere which intensified when substitute Terry Connor scored the winner with nine minutes remaining.

SATURDAY 24TH APRIL 1948

Millwall hammered the Sky Blues 6-2 at The Den in front of just over 12,000 south London supporters. Norman Lockhart and Ted Roberts netted consolation goals for Coventry who would win their last two games of the season with victories over Fulham and Chesterfield.

TUESDAY 24TH APRIL 1962

Highfield Road witnessed one of its best-ever debuts when Stuart Pearce donned the number three shirt. Signed by Bobby Gould from non-league Wealdstone for £25,000, Pearce took to the field against Queens Park Rangers and starred from the first minute. Born in Hammersmith, England's future left-back made just 54 first-team appearances before Brian Clough signed him for Nottingham Forest. He kept his nerve at the Victoria Ground, Stoke, to slam home the winning penalty prior to the magical wins over Luton Town and Everton that ensured survival. The Everton 4-1 win would be his last-ever game in sky blue.

SATURDAY 24TH APRIL 1976

David Cross ended the season as he started, with a hat-trick. Having won 4-1 at Goodison Park on the opening day, City beat Burnley 3-1 at Turf Moor. Not only did Cross take home the match ball, the game was the last match in the top flight for the hosts until 2009.

SATURDAY 25TH APRIL 1914

Prior to joining the Football League for the start of season 1919/20, the Sky Blues suffered relegation from Division One of the Southern League. A 1-1 draw at Highfield Road, with Norwich City the visitors on the final day of the season, ensured it would be Division Two for the Bantams, as City were known prior to Jimmy Hill's arrival.

SATURDAY 25TH APRIL 1959

Coventry ensured their Division Four tenure lasted just one season as promotion was secured with a 1-0 win over Watford at Highfield Road. Roy Kirk scored the goal which guaranteed promotion to Division Three in front of 13,434 supporters under Billy Frith's management. The title evaded City who claimed runners-up spot.

SATURDAY 25TH APRIL 1964

Coventry returned to Division Two as champions with a 1-0 win over Colchester United at Highfield Road. With injury having kept George Hudson out of the City line-up, Jimmy Hill ensured he was back for the vital game. Speaking to the *Daily Mirror* Hill said: "Three times I have asked George before if he felt fit to return. At last he agreed." Hudson's 23rd-minute goal ensured City took the title in front of 36,901 supporters. The side that day comprised Bob Wesson, John Sillett, Mick Kearns, Brian Hill, George Curtis, Ron Farmer, Willie Humphries, George Hudson, George Kirby, John Smith and Ronnie Rees.

TUESDAY 25TH APRIL 1967

The Sky Blues secured promotion to Division One without kicking a ball. Third-place Blackburn Rovers' failure to beat Bolton Wanderers sent Coventry and Wolverhampton Wanderers into the top flight four days prior to their clash at Highfield Road.

SATURDAY 25TH APRIL 1981

Following the decision to make Highfield Road an all-seater stadium at the beginning of season 1981/82, the Spion Kop made its farewell appearance (for the time being) with the visit of Southampton. The 18,242 crowd savoured their final standing appearance as Garry Thompson's second-half header took the two points for the Sky Blues.

WEDNESDAY 26TH APRIL 1944

Ernie Machin, who made 289 first-team appearances for the Sky Blues, was born in Walkden. Signed by Jimmy Hill, inside-forward Machin contributed to two promotions with 39 goals. He spent ten seasons with Coventry before moving to Plymouth Argyle in 1972. During the Division Two title-winning season, Machin scored 11 league goals including one in the final league game against Millwall that clinched the title.

MONDAY 27TH APRIL 1936

A 0-0 draw at Highfield Road against Luton Town set a new attendance record. A 42,975 crowd packed into the stadium with the Division Three (South) championship the prize. The point would take City into the final game a week later when victory over Torquay United would promote them to Division Two.

TUESDAY 27TH APRIL 1982

Garry Thompson and Mark Hateley scored two apiece as Sunderland were hammered 6-1 at Highfield Road. The scoreline was City's biggest win since they thrashed Shrewsbury Town 8-1 in October 1963. Gary Gillespie opened the scoring and Thompson soon made it two. Stan Cummins reduced the deficit by half-time before Hateley (two), Thompson again and Gerry Francis sent just 11,282 supporters away from Highfield Road having watched a feast of football.

SATURDAY 27TH APRIL 1996

With Premier League survival in the balance, the City hordes flocked to Selhurst Park for a must-win game against Wimbledon. On a warm day, the Sky Blues, weakened by injuries, scored two second-half goals to move themselves clear of danger. The 15,796 in attendance watched Peter Ndlovu fire in two of his most important Coventry goals to secure only the second away win all season.

SATURDAY 28TH APRIL 1934

Bristol-born Clarrie Bourton smashed home four goals as the Bantams recorded their highest-ever league victory with a 9-0 demolition of Bristol City at Highfield Road. Bourton's strikes took his season's total to 25 on his way to becoming the club's leading goalscorer of all time. Just 7,035 witnessed a team scoring feat yet to be broken up until season 2009/10.

SATURDAY 28TH APRIL 1984

Forever remembered for picking the ball out of the Crystal Palace net nine times at Anfield in September 1989, five years previously Perry Suckling suffered similar embarrassment. Aged just 19, Suckling conceded six second-half goals as Southampton destroyed Coventry with an 8-2 rout at The Dell. Danny Wallace and Steve Moran both scored hat-tricks as Saints finished runners-up to Liverpool by just three points.

WEDNESDAY 29TH APRIL 1908

Coventry beat West Bromwich Albion reserves 11-2 in a Birmingham & District League match at Highfield Road. Billy Smith scored five times and Albert Lewis twice as Joe Beaman's side finished the season in fourth position with 97 goals scored.

MONDAY 29TH APRIL 1957

Although he never played a first-team game, David Icke signed for the Sky Blues at the age of 15. Born in Leicester, arthritis put a gradual stop to his promising career and he was forced into retirement at just 21. A career in sports presenting followed before he proclaimed live on *Wogan* to millions of viewers that he was indeed the 'Son of God'.

SATURDAY 29TH APRIL 1967

Jimmy Hill dubbed the game 'Midlands Match of the Century'. Derek Henderson, then football correspondent for the *Coventry Evening Telegraph*, wrote: "Those who were there will never forget it. Nor perhaps, will they ever be able to convince those who were not of the unforgettable drama and electricity, of the greatest day in Highfield Road's history." Hill himself said after the game: "This was my magic moment. When one of the players tossed his shirt to the crowd, I told the others to do the same. I thought it was a nice gesture to a wonderful set of fans." Having secured promotion to Division One just four days earlier, 51,452 spectators created a new Highfield Road attendance record as the Sky Blues took on Wolverhampton Wanderers. With both teams already promoted the result would go a major way to determining the champions of Division Two. Peter Knowles opened the scoring for the visitors who led at the interval. Second-half goals from Ernie Machin, Ian Gibson and Ronnie Rees secured a 3-1 win, and one hand on the Division Two title.

SATURDAY 29TH APRIL 1978

Sixty seconds after Joe Royle had given Bristol City the lead, Ian Wallace levelled as a 1-1 draw at Ashton Gate would see the Sky Blues finish in 7th position. Wallace's strike was his 23rd of the season, 21 of them in the league, and contributed to the 75 goals the Sky Blues scored during season 1977/78.

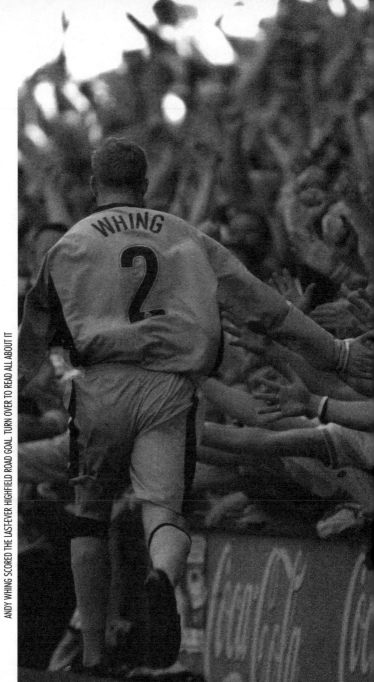

SATURDAY 30TH APRIL 1932

Leading goalscorer of all time, Clarrie Bourton, scored his seventh hat-trick of an amazing season as City beat Watford 5-0 at Highfield Road. He would end with 49 league goals and one in the FA Cup, a never-surpassed 50 goals in one Coventry City season, 1931/32.

WEDNESDAY 30TH APRIL 1958

Brian Hill, aged 16 years and 273 days, became the youngest player to start a match for the club in the 3-2 defeat at Gillingham. Hill scored on his debut and went on to make 286 first-team appearances, scoring eight goals in 14 seasons.

SATURDAY 30TH APRIL 2005

Highfield Road hosted its final Football League game with the visit of Derby County. Home to the Sky Blues since 1899, the stadium had been sold to McLean Homes back in December 1999 in preparation for the move to the Ricoh Arena. A crowd of 22,777 packed into the ground way before kick off to savour the great old ground for the final time. Jimmy Hill led the crowd in a rendition of the Sky Blue song prior to the players' arrival. What must not be forgotten is the Sky Blues needed a win, sat in 19th position prior to kick off. With the score 4-0 at half-time, goals from Gary McSheffrey (two), Dele Adebola and Stern John against fifth-placed Derby made for a carnival final 45 minutes. A second for John made it 5-2 but the introduction of right-back Andrew Whing capped the day in perfect style. His first touch flashed a half volley into the top corner of the net and placed him in the record books as the last-ever goalscorer at a wonderful football ground. City fan Gary McSheffrey spoke to the *Daily Mirror* after the game: "The way the goals went in during the first half was incredible – it must have been a great game for the fans and we could not have asked for a better day. We have got the support to create a Premiership atmosphere and hopefully when we get the new arena we can push for promotion." After the game Jimmy Hill appeared in the directors' box for one final time to again lead the singing to a packed stadium.

COVENTRY CITY
On This Day

MAY

THURSDAY 1st MAY 1980

Highfield Road hosted its first-ever FA Cup semi-final as Arsenal and Liverpool met for the fourth time to secure a place at Wembley. A crowd of 35,632 packed into the stadium to watch Brian Talbot take Arsenal to the Twin Towers with a 12th-minute goal. The previous ties at Hillsborough and Villa Park (twice) had failed to separate them and Arsenal would lose 1-0 to Division Two West Ham United in the showpiece final.

SATURDAY 1st MAY 2004

After just 20 games in charge, Eric Black was sacked as Coventry City manager following a 5-2 win at Gillingham. Black encouraged attacking football and was relieved of his duties as the club sat in 12th position. Peter Reid took over as manager for the final game at home to Crystal Palace. Black has since assisted Steve Bruce at Birmingham City, Wigan Athletic and Sunderland. During his spell in the hot-seat he won nine out of 18 games with two draws along the way.

SATURDAY 2nd MAY 1936

A crowd of 30,514 packed into Highfield Road to see the Sky Blues defeat Torquay United 2-1 and seal the Division Three (South) championship. Torquay took the lead with just 15 minutes remaining following George McNestry's penalty miss. Ernie Curtis succeeded where McNestry failed to level the score before Clarrie Bourton scored the winner with 88 minutes on the clock.

SATURDAY 2nd MAY 1981

Gordon Milne's final game as Sky Blues' manager was a visit to Brian Clough's Nottingham Forest. Garry Thompson opened the scoring before a John Robertson penalty levelled matters. Coventry ended the season in 16th position, 13 defeats away from home a major contributor. Milne took charge in 1972 and nine seasons later he moved to the position of general manager before taking over at Leicester City. Under his management, the Sky Blues reached the League Cup semi-final and finished seventh in 1978/79. He put in place the successful youth policy that produced the likes of Mark Hateley, Thompson, Gary Gillespie and Danny Thomas.

SATURDAY 2ND MAY 1981

A product of the Sky Blues' youth policy, Chris Kirkland made his debut against Tranmere Rovers in the Worthington Cup aged just 18 years old. Born in Barwell, Kirkland played 29 first-team matches for Coventry before his fine form prompted Liverpool to pay £6.5 million in August 2001. In 2006, he came on as substitute for his only full England cap, a friendly against Greece.

SATURDAY 2ND MAY 1992

Having taken over from Terry Butcher, Don Howe's final match in charge saw City rely on already relegated Notts County to stay in Division One. The Sky Blues lost 2-0 at Aston Villa as Notts County beat Luton Town 2-1 at Meadow Lane to preserve their status.

SUNDAY 2ND MAY 2010

Chris Coleman's final match as Coventry manager saw Watford win 4-0 at the Ricoh Arena in the last game of season 2009/10. The Sky Blues ended the campaign without a win in 11 matches and chairman Ray Ranson saw fit to relieve the former Welsh international of his managerial duties.

SATURDAY 3RD MAY 1980

Just three days after beating Liverpool 1-0 at Highfield Road in the FA Cup semi-final replay, the Gunners returned to take the two points as City ended the season eight points clear of the drop zone. Paul Vaessen's winner with two minutes remaining took the points for Arsenal.

SATURDAY 3RD MAY 1986

With George Curtis and John Sillett in charge, season 1985/86 went to the final game. Queens Park Rangers, safe in 13th position, visited Highfield Road. John Byrne's first-half goal increased the pressure with eyes and ears on the happenings at Ipswich Town and Oxford United. A Brian Kilcline special, hammered home from just outside the penalty area – combined with a Dave Bennett strike – took the Sky Blues into the break 2-1 ahead. Rangers hit the woodwork as their pressure so very nearly told; results elsewhere took Ipswich into Division Two with Birmingham City and West Bromwich Albion.

TUESDAY 4TH MAY 1982

Southampton and the Sky Blues drew a marvellous game of football 5-5 at The Dell as 18,522 watched City lead 2-1 at half-time. Goals from Steve Whitton and Mark Hateley sandwiched a Kevin Keegan strike. Keith Cassells levelled before Hateley made it 3-2, quickly added to by Whitton on the hour. In 22 crazy minutes, Alan Ball, Cassells and Keegan turned the tables on Coventry. With seven minutes remaining Southampton unbelievably led 5-4. Enter Mark Hateley to complete his hat-trick with 90 minutes on the clock to salvage a well deserved point.

FRIDAY 5TH MAY 1939

One of Coventry City's greatest-ever central defenders and captains, George Curtis was born in Dover. Only Steve Ogrizovic made more first-team appearances for the Sky Blues than 'The Ironman'. Between 1956 and 1969, Curtis appeared in first-team action on 543 occasions, scoring 13 goals. Division Three and Division Two titles were secured under his leadership before a broken leg in City's second Division One match at the City Ground sidelined him for the whole season. Later appointed managing director at Coventry City, he stepped up to managerial duties alongside John Sillett to mastermind the Wembley success following the resignation of Don Mackay.

SUNDAY 5TH MAY 1991

Liverpool had already won the Division One title prior to visiting Highfield Road. Nine points clear of Aston Villa they turned on the style to win 6-1 in front of 23,204 supporters. Kevin Gallacher opened the scoring before Ian Rush, Ronnie Rosenthal (two) and a hat-trick from John Barnes showed their class. Coventry's heaviest home defeat was consigned to the record books after the final whistle.

SUNDAY 5TH MAY 1996

Yet another last-day survival occurred at Highfield Road with the visit of Leeds United. Goal difference would keep the Sky Blues in the Premier League at the expense of Manchester City. Coventry drew 0-0 as the Mancunians fought back from two down to draw 2-2 at home to Liverpool. Soon to be sky blue, Gary McAllister played his last match for Leeds United before his £3 million transfer to Highfield Road.

SATURDAY 5TH MAY 2001

The most painful relegation the club has ever suffered saw Aston Villa claw back a two-goal deficit to win 3-2 at Villa Park. Coventry were relegated from the Premier League with one game to play; eight wins all season proved not enough to save the proud record of 34 unbroken top-flight years. Results elsewhere ensured even if the Sky Blues had beaten Aston Villa it was immaterial. At the time, with a 2-0 lead, there was hope. Moustapha Hadji scored twice with just 25 minutes on the clock. Darius Vassell, Juan Pablo Angel and Paul Merson ensured that with five minutes to play it was all over.

SATURDAY 5TH MAY 2007

Lee Hildreth holds the record for the shortest-ever Sky Blues career. With City leading Burnley 2-1 at Turf Moor, Iain Dowie sent on the youngster for a one-minute appearance to take the sting out of the home team's pressing for a late equaliser. Chris Coleman released him in the summer of 2008.

SATURDAY 6TH MAY 1944

The final game of Wartime League season 1943/44 attracted just 1,775 supporters as the Bantams beat Notts County 8-2. Goals from Barratt (four), McKeown (two), Crawley and Coen ended the campaign on a high.

MONDAY 7TH MAY 1962

Signed from Notts County by Bobby Gould, Brian Kilcline was the captain who lifted the FA Cup at Wembley on City's greatest day. Born in Nottingham, Kilcline went on to make 213 first-team appearances and scored 35 goals, many of them penalties blasted in with his trademark power. His partnership with Trevor Peake ensured the Sky Blues centre-half pairing was one of the best for seven seasons, the Wembley final one of their best-ever days. Terry Butcher's arrival signalled the end of his Coventry career as he was sold to Oldham Athletic. Further moves took him to Newcastle United, Swindon Town, Mansfield Town and Halifax Town. Following retirement Kilcline and his wife, Lynn, took off on a round-the-world ticket documented in their book titled *The Lion, The Witch and The Rucksack*.

MONDAY 7TH MAY 1984

Five years before he conceded nine in front of the Kop, Perry Suckling picked the ball out of the Sky Blues' net on five occasions. Ian Rush scored four times as Liverpool closed in on yet another title with a 5-0 win. Alan Hansen scored a rare goal as Coventry remained in 19th position with just one game to play.

SATURDAY 8TH MAY 1982

Just four days after the ten-goal thriller at The Dell, the Sky Blues turned on the style again at Maine Road. Following his double against Southampton, Steve Whitton smashed a hat-trick past Alex Williams to give Coventry an unassailable 3-0 lead before Trevor Francis added respectability. Former Sky Blue Bobby McDonald was powerless to stop Whitton firing in his treble as he powered down the Manchester City left side.

SATURDAY 8TH MAY 1993

A crowd of 19,571 bode farewell to the Spion Kop after a thrilling 3-3 draw with Leeds United. The new East Stand construction would see Coventry play in a three-sided stadium during season 1993/94. City led 3-1 with a minute left on the clock before a Rod Wallace double levelled the score for ten-man Leeds. Having won the title the previous May, Leeds were unable to win away from Elland Road all season.

SUNDAY 9TH MAY 1971

Upon signing Don Hutchison on loan from Millwall, manager Micky Adams, speaking to the *Coventry Evening Telegraph*, said: "There's a saying that class is permanent and that applies to Don. He may not have the legs he had when he was younger but he possesses a fantastic ability to read the game." Born in Gateshead on this day, Hutchison made his Sky Blues debut as substitute in a 2-2 home draw with Norwich City in November 2005. His 15 first-team appearances, with 25 as substitute, highlighted the cameo role he performed. He scored four goals, most memorably the Goal of The Season at Elland Road, struck on the half volley from 25 yards, past Neil Sullivan.

BRIAN KILCLINE — COVENTRY CITY'S FA CUP-WINNING CAPTAIN

SUNDAY 9TH MAY 2004

Appointed by Mike McGinnity to replace the sacked Eric Black, Peter Reid's first game as Sky Blues manager inspired a 2-1 win over soon-to-be-promoted Crystal Palace. The largest crowd of the season, 22,202, applauded Coventry off the field after finishing the season in 12th position. Mo Konjic and Michael Doyle fired City into a 2-0 half-time lead before Dougie Freedman pulled one back for Iain Dowie's side. The visitors would seal promotion to the Premier League at Wembley just three weeks later.

SUNDAY 10TH MAY 1987

It was confirmed that the knee injury sustained by Brian Borrows in the final game of the season would keep him out of the Wembley showpiece. Twisting awkwardly on the Highfield Road turf, Borrows limped out of the game and out of the club's greatest day. The 1-1 draw with Southampton was notable for yet another Brian Kilcline free kick spectacular but more for the sheer bad luck suffered by Coventry's 'Mr Consistent'.

SATURDAY 11TH MAY 1991

Champions Arsenal turned on the style with a thumping 6-1 win at Highbury. With 12 minutes remaining the Sky Blues were trailing 2-1 before Anders Limpar cut loose to claim the match ball. A Trevor Peake own goal, and strikes from Alan Smith and Perry Groves completed the rout while Kevin Gallacher scored for Coventry.

SUNDAY 11TH MAY 1997

Coventry's 2-1 win at White Hart Lane to yet again stave off relegation can be considered the greatest escape of them all. Sunderland's defeat and Middlesbrough's draw at Leeds United kept the Sky Blues in the Premier League by just one point. The game kicked off 15 minutes late, mirroring the Bristol City game in 1977. Dion Dublin and Paul Williams launched City into a two-goal lead before Paul McVeigh made the half-time score 2-1. A wonderful save from Steve Ogrizovic foiled the same player as Coventry held on to secure an unbelievable win.

SATURDAY 12TH MAY 1984

As the clock ticked onto 70 minutes the Sky Blues were on their way to Division Two. Enter Dave Bennett to score direct from a corner past England goalkeeper Chris Woods. Future Sky Blue Robert Rosario then headed a cross against Perry Suckling's post with four minutes to play. On loan Mick Ferguson had earlier scored his third goal in seven games to aid the rescue act after John Deehan's opener for Norwich City.

WEDNESDAY 13TH MAY 1987

The Sky Blues' squad, resplendent in their Cup Final tracksuits, appeared on *Blue Peter* to sing their cup song Go For It City! live on tea time television. Coventry supporters Steve and Heather Taylor wrote the song which peaked at number 61 in the UK singles chart.

THURSDAY 14TH MAY 1970

One of the most popular post Premiership Coventry players, Mo Konjic, was born in Tuzla, Bosnia. Signed by Gordon Strachan, Konjic made his debut in February 1999 in a 0-0 draw with Tottenham Hotspur at White Hart Lane. During his Sky Blues career he made 155 first-team appearances and scored four goals. 'Big Mo' returned to Highfield Road with his new side, Derby County, to a standing ovation prior to City's 6-2 demolition in the final ever game at the ground.

SATURDAY 14TH MAY 1983

Dave Sexton's final match in charge of Coventry City welcomed West Ham United to Highfield Road. With no threat of relegation the Sky Blues lost 4-2 as John Hendrie and Steve Whitton scored for Coventry. This game saw the demise of Sexton's young side as Sealey, Thomas, Gillespie, Dyson, Whitton and Hateley played their last game in Sky Blue.

SUNDAY 14TH MAY 2000

The Sky Blues' penultimate top-flight season saddled them with the unenviable record of failing to win an away game. A 1-0 defeat on the final day to already-relegated Watford put the seal on a disappointing year which saw their top-flight status preserved by virtue of winning 12 out of 19 home matches.

MONDAY 15TH MAY 1967

Coventry clinched the Division Two championship with a 3-1 win over Millwall at Highfield Road. Goals from John Tudor, Ernie Machin and John Key took the title as the jubilant chant of 'Champions, Champions' rang out around the stadium.

SATURDAY 15TH MAY 1982

Birmingham City visited on the final day with victory needed to preserve their top-flight status. The newly introduced three points for a win would keep them in the division at the expense of Leeds United. Future Sky Blue Mick Harford scored the winner on 86 minutes, causing pandemonium in the visitors' section.

SATURDAY 16TH MAY 1987

Coventry City Football Club's greatest day: 98,000 supporters witnessed a fantastic game of football as the Sky Blues twice came from behind to defeat Tottenham Hotspur 3-2 after extra time in the FA Cup Final. John Sillett and George Curtis took their places on the bench as Brian Kilcline introduced the City players to the royal party. Within two minutes, Clive Allen headed in Chris Waddle's cross for his 49th goal of a marvellous season. It took only seven minutes for Coventry to level as Dave Bennett rounded Ray Clemence to fire into an empty net. With three minutes to go until the interval, Hoddle's free kick was met by a combination of Gary Mabbutt and Brian Kilcline and the ball spun agonisingly into the corner of the net. Both sides continued to attack until a glorious moment occurred in the 63rd minute. Dave Bennett's fabulous cross was met by a diving Keith Houchen who propelled the ball into the corner of Ray Clemence's net to level at 2-2. Graham Rodger replaced the injured Brian Kilcline and it was his pass that created *that* magical moment. Finding himself on the right wing for possibly the only time in his career, Lloyd McGrath raced to the edge of the penalty area before crossing the ball. In slow motion, the ball deflected off Gary Mabbutt's knee to leave Clemence stranded as it arched into the far corner of the net. Coventry City 3 Tottenham Hotspur 2. Brian Kilcline then led the side up the Wembley steps to lift the famous trophy.

FRIDAY 17TH MAY 1985

The Sky Blues needed to win their remaining three games to stay in the top flight. Stuart Pearce's 66th-minute penalty handed lifeline number one against a Stoke team who lost 31 out of their 42 league games in a nightmare season. Referee Neil Midgley, who would referee the Wembley final, awarded Stoke a penalty with six minutes to play. Future City striker Iain Painter smashed his kick against the bar and Coventry survived.

SUNDAY 17TH MAY 1987

Speaking to the *Sunday Mirror*, cup hero Keith Houchen summed up the day: "Football has given me more than I could hope this year, and I can't complain about anything anymore." John Sillett was equally buoyant: "I knew Spurs didn't fancy extra time. Some of their heads had dropped."

FRIDAY 18TH MAY 2001

Coventry supporters prepared for their final Premier League game at Highfield Road. The visitors, Bradford City, were also relegated and both clubs could have done without the fixture. Manchester City would join them in Division One the following August.

THURSDAY 19TH MAY 1977

Both Coventry and Bristol City needed a result to stay up in the final game at Highfield Road. Traffic congestion ensured the game kicked off 15 minutes late and the Sky Blues swept into a two-goal lead, courtesy of Tommy Hutchison. The West Country side levelled through Gerry Gow and Don Gillies with 11 minutes remaining. With five minutes to play, Sunderland's defeat at Everton flashed up on the scoreboard which meant both sides were safe and an unofficial truce was declared.

THURSDAY 20TH MAY 2010

Aidy Boothroyd became the Sky Blues' ninth manager in as many years after signing a three-year contract. Speaking to Sky Sports he enthused: "This is a big club, and a big challenge, but it's one I am very much looking forward to. There is plenty of potential here. That comes from the financial stability and the magnificent ground. I'm looking forward to getting on with the job."

SATURDAY 21st MAY 2005

Stephen Hughes collected the Player of The Year and Players' Player of The Year awards at the end-of-season awards dinner. Andrew Whing's reward for scoring the last-ever professional goal at Highfield Road was Goal of The Season while Isaac Osbourne picked up Young Player of The Year.

THURSDAY 22nd MAY 2008

Signed by Iain Dowie in July 2007, Michael Hughes was released by Chris Coleman upon the expiration of his one-year contract. The former Northern Ireland international made 20 first-team appearances without scoring as he failed to feature from mid February onwards.

WEDNESDAY 23rd MAY 1956

Signed by Gordon Milne for £75,000 from Dumbarton, Ian Wallace made his debut as substitute in a 2-1 home defeat to Sunderland in October 1976. Born in Glasgow on this day, Wallace made 140 first-team appearances and scored 60 goals before Brian Clough signed him for European Cup winners Nottingham Forest. His strike partnership with Mick Ferguson took the Sky Blues to seventh place in 1977/78, and between them they scored 40 out of the 75 the side amassed in that excellent campaign. The 21 league-goal haul from Wallace is still a top-flight club record.

THURSDAY 23rd MAY 1985

Following the 1-0 win at Stoke City, lifeline number two arrived with just six minutes remaining against Luton Town. With such an important game the ball boys were replaced by youth team players so the ball could be returned at the earliest opportunity. A corner from the right side was cleared as far as Brian Kilcline who volleyed into the corner of Les Sealey's goal. There was absolute pandemonium as the goal went in, followed shortly afterwards by the final whistle.

SATURDAY 24th MAY 2008

Hull City beat Bristol City 1-0 at Wembley to secure promotion to the Premier League in the play-off final. Former Sky Blues Dele Adebola and Louis Carey lined up for the Robins alongside future Coventry left winger Michael McIndoe.

MONDAY 25TH MAY 1942

Coventry played their first game since the outbreak of World War II against Birmingham City. A friendly game, the gate receipts went to charitable causes. A crowd of 5,491 watched the Bantams win 4-2 with Leslie Jones and Tommy Crawley both notching doubles.

SUNDAY 26TH MAY 1968

The only member of the FA Cup-winning squad not to step on the Wembley turf, Steve Sedgley was born in Enfield. An unused substitute on the big day, Sedgley made his debut against Arsenal in a 2-1 win at Highfield Road in August 1987. He made 103 first-team appearances for the Sky Blues and scored five goals. In the summer of 1989 he transferred to Tottenham Hotspur for £750,000.

SUNDAY 26TH MAY 1985

Lifeline number three miraculously arrived on a gloriously sunny Sunday morning at Highfield Road. Household names Southall, Van den Hauwe, Ratcliffe, Richardson, Steven, Sharp, Bracewell and Sheedy were destroyed 4-1 by a rampant Sky Blues in an 11.30am kick off. A season's best 21,596 raised the roof as goals from Cyrille Regis (two), Micky Adams and Terry Gibson relegated Norwich City into Division Two.

MONDAY 27TH MAY 1985

Following the dramatic 4-1 win over Everton, Cyrille Regis emerged as the hero after his two goals saved the Sky Blues from relegation. Three goals in 31 appearances prior to the game had not set the season alight as Regis admitted to the *Daily Mirror*: "This has to be one of the most satisfying days of my career. I've had something of a nightmare time here and I was aware that if we had gone down the fans would have blamed me for my lack of goals. And they would have been right."

TUESDAY 28TH MAY 1985

Just two days after survival was guaranteed, Brian Clough signed Stuart Pearce and Ian Butterworth for Nottingham Forest in a double deal worth £450,000. Pearce would become captain and lead the East Midlands side to numerous Wembley cup finals over a 12-year stay.

FRIDAY 29TH MAY 1987

The play-offs were introduced for season 1986/87 and added an extra dimension to the relegation/promotion issues in the respective divisions. Charlton Athletic became the first winners as they defeated Leeds United 2-1 after extra time at St. Andrew's, home of Birmingham City. Former Sky Blues Bobby McDonald and Micky Adams lined up for Leeds United while Jim Melrose led the Charlton Athletic attack.

MONDAY 30TH MAY 1994

Future Coventry centre-half Paul Williams was on the losing side as Derby County lost 1-0 to Leicester City in the play-off final at Wembley. Williams joined the Sky Blues in the summer of 1995 and would suffer relegation from the Premier League in 2001. In over six seasons he played 199 first-team games and scored six goals in sky blue.

MONDAY 30TH MAY 2005

Former Sky Blue Robbie Keane, now leading the attack of Tottenham Hotspur, sang the praises of incoming Celtic manager Gordon Strachan. Speaking to *The Independent* Keane said: "I'm sure he's going to do a tremendous job – he gets the best out of players and knows the game inside out. I'm a Celtic fan and I have said that one day I would like to play for them."

TUESDAY 31ST MAY 2005

Gordon Strachan prepared for the start of life as Celtic manager by renewing the acquaintance of his former assistant Gary Pendrey. Pendrey worked with Strachan throughout his time as Sky Blues' manager and followed him to Southampton.

SATURDAY 31ST MAY 2008

Coventry City directors and fellow businessmen led the tributes to Joe Elliott at a luncheon for him yesterday. Joe was honoured for the work he undertook in saving the club from administration and getting the go ahead for the takeover led by Ray Ranson. Council chief John McGuigan spoke to the *Coventry Evening Telegraph*: "There is a huge admiration and affection in Coventry for Joe Elliott. I've never heard anyone say anything negative about him. Whilst everyone associates Joe with the football club, this is just a small part of the contribution he has made to Coventry."

COVENTRY CITY
On This Day

JUNE

THURSDAY 1st JUNE 1950

Signed by Gordon Milne from German side Cologne, Roger Van Gool was born in Nieuwmoer, Belgium. He made his debut in a 2-0 home defeat to West Bromwich Albion at Highfield Road having signed for £250,000, and plied his trade down the right wing with his socks rolled down to his ankles. In the two seasons he spent at Coventry, the Belgian made only 19 first-team appearances and failed to find the net.

SUNDAY 2nd JUNE 2002

Prior to leaving the Sky Blues for Celtic in the summer of 2002, Magnus Hedman represented Sweden in the World Cup Group F game at the Saitama Stadium in Saitama. A crowd of 52,721 watched Sweden's 1-1 draw with England as Sol Campbell's opener was cancelled out by Niclas Alexandersson.

TUESDAY 3rd JUNE 1986

England's shock 1-0 defeat to Portugal in their opening group game of the 1986 World Cup finals saw past and future Sky Blues in action. Mark Hateley had departed for Portsmouth in the summer of 1983 whilst Kenny Sansom, Peter Reid and Terry Butcher would all play their part in the future of the club in years to come.

WEDNESDAY 4th JUNE 1997

Simon Haworth joined the Sky Blues from Cardiff City for a fee of £500,000. A centre forward, Haworth played second fiddle to Huckerby and Dublin and made only 14 first-team appearances, the majority as substitute, and scored one goal in a 4-1 Carling Cup win over Everton in October 1997. He retired through injury in 2004 after more fruitful spells at Wigan Athletic and Tranmere Rovers.

WEDNESDAY 5th JUNE 2002

Voted third-best Coventry City Player of the Top-Flight era, Robbie Keane spent just under one season at Highfield Road. Even though he left the club in August 2001, he remains hugely popular and scored the added-time equaliser for the Republic of Ireland in their 1-1 draw with Germany in the 2002 World Cup Group E encounter.

THURSDAY 6TH JUNE 2002

Khalilou Fadiga made just one first-team appearance and five as substitute during a four-month spell with the Sky Blues in early 2007. Signed by Iain Dowie, Fadiga was released at the end of the season and moved to Belgian side Gent. On this day, Fadiga wore the number ten shirt for Senegal in their 1-1 draw with Denmark at the 2002 World Cup.

TUESDAY 7TH JUNE 1938

Ian St. John, who made his Coventry debut in a 1-0 win against Tottenham Hotspur at Highfield Road in September 1971, was born in Motherwell. The 'Saint' played just 22 first-team games for the Sky Blues and scored three goals. He joined the club aged 33 under the stewardship of Noel Cantwell, but the appointments of Gordon Milne and Joe Mercer as joint managers saw St. John move to Tranmere Rovers where he closed his playing career.

SUNDAY 7TH JUNE 1981

Born in Stranraer on this day, Kevin Kyle joined the Sky Blues from Sunderland for £600,000 in August 2006. Speaking to BBC Sport, manager Micky Adams was delighted with the signing: "Kevin provides an obvious aerial threat, as well as being very strong on the ball. He is a proven goalscorer at this level and he has also experienced football on the international stage, which can only be of benefit." Kyle scored on his debut against Norwich City in a 3-0 win at the Ricoh Arena. His performance was outstanding that day but over the course of the next two seasons he managed only four more goals in 47 first-team appearances.

MONDAY 8TH JUNE 1936

Willie Humphries cost Jimmy Hill £5,000 in May 1962 when he signed from Ards. A lightning quick winger with an excellent delivery, Humphries made 126 first-team appearances and scored 24 goals. Born on this day in Ards, Northern Ireland, he was a key part of the Division Three championship-winning side and won 14 Northern Ireland caps during his career. Jimmy Hill later sold him to Swansea where he spent three seasons before returning to Ards and a career in management.

SUNDAY 9TH JUNE 1912

Billy Frith played for and managed Coventry City. A wing half, he played alongside Clarrie Bourton and Jock Lauderdale in Harry Storer's free-scoring side of the early to mid 1930s. Frith, who made 177 first-team appearances and scored four goals for the Bantams before turning his hand to management, was born in Sheffield on this day. He took over as Coventry manager in June 1947 and was responsible for the signing of Reg Matthews; but his tenure was short. With City in the bottom two in November 1948 Frith was sacked. A second spell as manager commenced in September 1957 and promotion from Division Four followed in 1959. Frith's final game in charge was the humiliating 2-1 defeat to non-league Kings Lynn at Highfield Road in November 1961. City chairman, Derrick Robins, appointed Jimmy Hill as his successor.

TUESDAY 9TH JUNE 2009

The *Coventry Evening Telegraph* reported the staggering success of Take That's first of three live shows at the Ricoh Arena. Around 38,000 fans packed the stadium to watch Gary, Mark, Howard and Jason perform their *Circus Live* show. The tour sold 35 million tickets in just one day and broke all box-office records for the 14-date stadium tour.

SATURDAY 10TH JUNE 1961

Signed by Bobby Gould in the summer of 1983 from Bristol Rovers, Nicky Platnauer was born in Leicester. He appeared 53 times for the Sky Blues' first team and scored six goals. Platnauer is famously remembered for stooping low to head into the Liverpool net after just 45 seconds in the fantastic 4-0 win at Highfield Road in December 1983. At the end of his first season in sky blue, he was voted Player of the Year by the supporters. After leaving Highfield Road in December 1984, he moved to Birmingham City, Cardiff City, Notts County, Leicester City, Scunthorpe United, Mansfield Town and Lincoln City and appeared at Wembley in three play-off finals, two with Leicester and one with Notts County. Since 2007 he has been assistant manager at Hinckley United in the Conference North.

WEDNESDAY 10TH JUNE 1970

Previous Coventry manager Chris Coleman was born in Swansea on this day. As a player, Coleman made just shy of 500 first-team appearances for Swansea City, Crystal Palace, Blackburn Rovers and Fulham. He found the net on 23 occasions adding 32 caps for Wales along the way. Following a successful spell at Fulham with Kevin Keegan, he moved into management with the west London side before moving to Real Sociedad in Spain. Sky Blues' chairman Ray Ranson signed him on a three-and-a-half year contract in February 2008 to replace Iain Dowie.

TUESDAY 11TH JUNE 2002

Former Sky Blue players Robbie Keane and Gary Breen both scored in the Group E game against Saudi Arabia in the 2002 World Cup. A crowd of 65,320 were in the International Stadium, Yokohama to see the Republic of Ireland qualify for the knockout phase with a 3-0 win.

WEDNESDAY 12TH JUNE 1946

After 42 goals in 89 games for Coventry City, Jimmy Hill justified his decision to sell fans' favourite George Hudson and replace him with Bobby Gould. Gould, who scored 24 times as the Sky Blues won the Division Two title in season 1966/67, was born in Coventry. He scored eight goals in 13 Division One matches before he was sold to Arsenal in January 1968. In 1983, Gould replaced Dave Sexton as Coventry manager and signed the likes of Steve Ogrizovic, Trevor Peake, Brian Kilcline, Terry Gibson and Stuart Pearce before his departure in December 1984. He returned for the start of the Premier League in August 1992 when City became the inaugural leaders but resigned in October 1993 after a 5-1 reverse at Queens Park Rangers.

SUNDAY 12TH JUNE 1960

Sky Blues chairman, Ray Ranson, was born in St. Helens on this day. His playing career began in 1978 and saw him top 400 appearances. Manchester City was his first club; one of the highlights saw him provide the cross for Tommy Hutchison's diving header in the 1981 FA Cup Final. As head of the takeover which saved Coventry from administration in December 2007, Ranson's business acumen and football knowledge has proved invaluable in restructuring the massive debt he encountered upon his arrival.

MONDAY 13TH JUNE 2005

Sky Blues chairman Mike McGinnity wanted to know if injury-prone midfielder Tim Sherwood had found alternative employment. Signed by Peter Reid, he made just 11 first-team appearances before an old ankle injury prevented him from playing. Speaking to the *Coventry Evening Telegraph*, McGinnity said: "I will be talking to Tim and hoping to sort something out with him. If he is going to be in the first-team squad then fine, if not, we have to discuss the situation further. I am sure the manager will be able to assess whether he is fit and whether or not his heart is in the club."

FRIDAY 14TH JUNE 1974

Sky Blues winger Tommy Hutchison came on as substitute for Kenny Dalglish in Scotland's 2-0 win over Zaire in the 1974 World Cup. Scotland led 2-0 when Hutchison was introduced after 75 minutes.

THURSDAY 15TH JUNE 2006

Soon to be sky blue, Chris Birchall, lined up alongside Coventry striker, Stern John, in Trinidad and Tobago's 2-0 defeat against England in the 2006 World Cup. A crowd of 41,000 saw late goals from Peter Crouch and Steven Gerrard in the Stadion Nurnberg clinch progress to the knockout phase.

TUESDAY 16TH JUNE 1970

Cobi Jones, who made his Coventry debut in a 2-1 win over Leeds United at Highfield Road in September 1994, was born in Detroit. Signed by Phil Neal for £300,000, Jones stayed until the end of the season when Ron Atkinson released him. His 25 first-team appearances brought him two goals; one at Highfield Road and one at Selhurst Park in Phil Neal's final match in charge.

MONDAY 16TH JUNE 2003

The Coventry City Masters side lost out in the Midland section heats despite not losing on the day. Three draws against Leicester City, Norwich City and Ipswich Town at the Skydome were not enough to secure a place in the finals.

SUNDAY 17TH JUNE 1990

Jose Perdomo, who joined Coventry three months after the 1990 World Cup finals, lined up against Belgium in the Uruguayans' 3-1 defeat during the group stage.

THURSDAY 18TH JUNE 1992

Sky Blues' striker Kevin Gallacher lined up for Scotland in their European Championship Group 2 game against the Ukraine. Scotland won 3-0 with goals from Paul McStay, Gary McAllister and Brian McClair.

WEDNESDAY 18TH JUNE 2008

Kieren Westwood signed for Coventry City from Carlisle United on a three-year contract. Having played over 120 first-team matches for the Cumbrians, Westwood joined Coventry to replace Andy Marshall.

THURSDAY 18TH JUNE 2009

Having joined the Sky Blues from Cambridge United in the summer of 2007, Robbie Simpson made 71 first-team appearances and scored seven goals. He joined Huddersfield Town for a fee in the region of £300,000 on a three-year contract.

FRIDAY 19TH JUNE 2009

Icelandic long throw expert Aron Gunnarsson was the subject of speculation linking him with a £5 million move to Liverpool. Having enjoyed an outstanding first season in English football, he collected the Player of the Year award and looked forward to building on his success in the following campaign.

FRIDAY 20TH JUNE 2003

The Sky Blues' new super stadium was facing yet another delay as the blame shifted onto the original contractors pulling out of the project. Under the new timetable, the 32,000-seater stadium would now be complete by December 2004 and should open in January 2005 after health and safety checks. Council leader, John Mutton, speaking to the *Coventry Evening Telegraph* said: "The original timetable to build and be open for the first game of the 2004 season was very tight. There was a danger that risks would be taken to meet it. This way, everything can be done in an open and transparent way."

SUNDAY 21st JUNE 1998

Former Coventry players Roy Wegerle and Cobi Jones lined up for the USA in their Group F 2-1 defeat to Iran in Lyon's Gerland stadium in the 1998 World Cup.

MONDAY 22nd JUNE 1998

Viorel Moldovan became the first Sky Blues player to score in a World Cup tournament. A crowd of 33,500 packed into the Stade de Toulouse to see Moldovan open the scoring against England in the 47th minute. Michael Owen levelled before Dan Petrescu scored the winner in the 90th minute to leave England needing a win in their final group game against Colombia to progress.

MONDAY 23rd JUNE 1975

Signed by Gary McAllister in the summer of 2003 along with Michael Doyle and Andy Morrell, Dele Adebola made 181 first-team appearances and scored 43 goals. Of his appearances, 53 were as substitute, a Coventry record. Born in Lagos, Nigeria on this day, Adebola scored in both the last game at Highfield Road and the first game at the Ricoh Arena.

TUESDAY 23rd JUNE 1998

Sky Blues past and present lined up in the Stade Geoffroy-Guichard in St. Etienne as Morocco defeated Scotland 3-0 in a Group A match at the World Cup. Colin Hendry and Kevin Gallacher started for Scotland while Youssef Chippo and Moustapha Hadji inspired the Moroccans to victory.

TUESDAY 24th JUNE 2008

Bon Jovi sold out the Ricoh Arena as part of their Lost Highway tour which took in such venues as St. Mary's stadium, Hampden Park, City of Manchester stadium, Ashton Gate and Twickenham.

TUESDAY 25th JUNE 1946

Born in Milnrow, Lancashire, Chris Cattlin joined the Sky Blues from Huddersfield Town in 1968 under the management of Noel Cantwell. A left-back, Cattlin never scored for Coventry in 239 first-team appearances over nine seasons. He moved to Brighton & Hove Albion upon his release in the summer of 1976 and eventually managed the club in 1983.

THURSDAY 25th JUNE 2009

Following the release of the forthcoming season's fixtures, the local police moved swiftly to move the kick off to 12.30pm for the visit of Leicester City. The previous season's game was blighted by hooliganism in Earlsdon high street as supporters ran riot.

MONDAY 26th JUNE 2006

The overspend on the Ricoh Arena totalled £5.4 million. Deputy council leader, Tony O'Neill, spoke to the *Coventry Evening Telegraph*: "Looking at projects of equal size across the country, given that most projects overspend by twenty per cent, to come in at this level is good news for us. It was originally £113.3 million and now its £118.7 million. Of course, we are not happy this has come out of council coffers but given the size of the project, I believe it is worth it."

WEDNESDAY 27th JUNE 2001

Having joined Coventry for a club-record fee of £6.5 million just ten months previously, Craig Bellamy moved on in the summer after relegation. Newcastle United ensured the Sky Blues recouped the £6.5 million paid to Norwich City as Bobby Robson snapped up the Welsh international. The funds would be used to acquire Lee Hughes and Keith O'Neill as the club prepared for life outside the top flight.

MONDAY 27th JUNE 2005

Richard Shaw and Trevor Benjamin agreed one-year deals with Coventry as Micky Adams moved to snap up the long-serving defender and journeyman striker. Shaw joined the club in 1995 so the year-long deal would see him through his testimonial season.

FRIDAY 27th JUNE 2008

Right-sided midfielder, Ellery Cairo, left the Sky Blues for Dutch side NAC Breda upon the expiry of his one-year contract. Signed by Iain Dowie from Hertha Berlin on a free transfer, Cairo made just nine first-team appearances without scoring. Chris Coleman chose not to renew the player's contract upon his arrival.

TUESDAY 28TH JUNE 1994

Sky Blues' centre-half Phil Babb wore the number 14 shirt for the Republic of Ireland in their Group E 0-0 draw with Norway at the 1994 World Cup. A crowd of 72,404 watched in the Giants Stadium, New York as the Irish qualified for the knockout phase. Babb had an outstanding tournament and transferred to Liverpool three games into the new season.

SATURDAY 28TH JUNE 2008

The *Express & Star* reported Coventry as close to sealing the signing of Wolverhampton Wanderers striker, Freddy Eastwood. Both clubs had been haggling over the deal for many weeks and a breakthrough seemed close. Eastwood himself said: "I don't want to be going back to Wolves knowing I'm not going to play."

FRIDAY 29TH JUNE 2007

Coventry were in a three-horse race to sign Blackburn Rovers' centre-half, Andy Todd. Todd's agent, Peter Harrison, spoke to the *Coventry Evening Telegraph*: "I have spoken to three clubs about Andy, who are all in England; two in the Premiership and one in the Championship." Todd eventually signed for Derby County and was a part of their infamous Premier League season where only one win was forthcoming.

FRIDAY 30TH JUNE 1967

David Busst, who joined Coventry from non-league Moor Green, was born in Birmingham. Following his retirement Busst continued to work for the club in the Football in the Community department of which he is now the director. After his horrendous leg break at Old Trafford the two sides met in a testimonial match on May 16th 1997 at Highfield Road. A full house gave him a fitting send off as Sir Alex Ferguson brought a full strength side to play the Sky Blues.

TUESDAY 30TH JUNE 2009

On September 26th 2007, he scored both goals at Old Trafford as the Sky Blues beat Manchester United in the third round of the Carling Cup. Today, the contract of Michael Mifsud ran its course and the diminutive striker was released into the football wilderness.

COVENTRY CITY
On This Day

JULY

SATURDAY 1st JULY 2000

Gary McAllister moved to Liverpool at the end of his four-year contract with the Sky Blues. Aged 35 at the time, the midfield playmaker would go on to play a major role in Liverpool's success. In season 2000/01 the Reds won the FA Cup, Uefa Cup and Worthington Cup with McAllister making 49 appearances, scoring seven goals. Coventry would end 2000/01 relegated to Division One, the absence of McAllister a major factor.

SUNDAY 2nd JULY 2006

A crowd of 40,000, some on the pitch, watched the Red Hot Chili Peppers entertain the Ricoh Arena masses. On a glorious summer day, the Chili Peppers followed in the footsteps of Bryan Adams and Bon Jovi in selling out the stadium.

SUNDAY 3rd JULY 2005

Stadium auctioneers SHM Smith Hodgkinson visited Highfield Road for an auction on the famous pitch. Hundreds of mementoes including the dugouts, ground signs, programme stands and turnstiles were up for grabs. Floodlights, seats, players' tunnel and furniture had already been up for tender in May and over £60,000 was raised.

SATURDAY 4th JULY 1998

Soon to be Sky Blue, Robert Jarni scored the opening goal for Croatia in their 3-0 World Cup quarter-final win over Germany. Goran Vlaovic and Davor Suker completed the scoring.

TUESDAY 5th JULY 1960

Born in Stirling on this day, Gary Gillespie joined the Sky Blues from Falkirk as a 17-year-old, signed by Gordon Milne. A cultured, ball playing centre-half, Gillespie made 205 first-team appearances and scored six goals before his departure to Liverpool in the summer of 1983. He became Joe Fagan's first signing for the Reds and went on to make over 150 appearances for them over eight seasons. Following three seasons at Celtic, Phil Neal re-signed him for Coventry in September 1994 but his stay was short and he went onto the coaching side in early 1995. During his time at Liverpool he collected 13 Scotland caps.

WEDNESDAY 5TH JULY 1961

Steve Jacobs came through the youth ranks at Coventry and made his debut in a 1-0 defeat to Arsenal at Highfield Road in the final game of season 1979/80. During his time at the club, Jacobs played in a variety of positions; either full-back, centre-half or central midfield. Born in West Ham, he made 115 first-team appearances and failed to score during his six seasons at the club.

THURSDAY 6TH JULY 1933

Frank Austin, who made 313 first-team appearances over ten seasons, was born in Stoke-on-Trent. Austin played under seven managers at Coventry before moving to Torquay United in January 1963.

MONDAY 7TH JULY 1986

Tony Dobson signed as a professional with Coventry City at 18 years old. A left-back, Dobson made his debut at Villa Park in March 1987 as the Sky Blues lost 1-0. He made 63 first-team appearances for his hometown club and scored a solitary goal in the 3-1 win over Everton in August 1990. In January 1991, along with Steve Livingstone, he transferred to Blackburn Rovers, signed by Kenny Dalglish.

TUESDAY 8TH JULY 1980

Robbie Keane, who joined the Sky Blues from Wolverhampton Wanderers for a then club record fee of £6 million, was born in Tallaght, Dublin. Two goals on his debut at home to Derby County ensured hero status from day one. Although he stayed less than a season, Keane scored 12 goals in 34 first-team appearances and entertained at all times. Inter Milan paid £13 million to take him to Italy in the summer of 2000. Voted the third best-ever Coventry player of the top flight era, he is one of the most popular players to wear sky blue.

SUNDAY 8TH JULY 2001

The 1987 FA Cup Final referee Neil Midgley died at his home in Kearsley, Bolton aged 58. On his first return to Highfield Road after the Wembley final in April 1988, the West Terrace chanted "One Neil Midgley, there's only one Neil Midgley!"

WEDNESDAY 9TH JULY 1986

Kevin Thornton, who made his Coventry debut as substitute against Crystal Palace at Selhurst Park in the League Cup second round, was born in Drogheda. September 2005 saw this prodigious talent introduced to City fans. Prior to his departure in July 2009 for off-field misdemeanours, Thornton made 55 first-team appearances and scored two goals, both away from home, and is now with Northampton Town.

SATURDAY 10TH JULY 1948

The third leading appearance maker for the Sky Blues was born in Grimsby on this day. Mick Coop made 492 first-team appearances between 1966 and his departure to Derby County in the summer of 1981. He returned to the club in 1985 as youth team coach and led them to Youth Cup glory just three days prior to the Wembley success with an extra-time victory over Charlton Athletic at Highfield Road.

SATURDAY 11TH JULY 1959

Bobby Gould signed Dave Bennett for £100,000 from Cardiff City in the summer of 1983. Over the next six seasons his wing play lit up Highfield Road as he made 209 first-team appearances and scored 35 goals. It was Bennett who inspired the semi-final comeback against Leeds United when he set up Michael Gynn after chasing a lost cause. During the final, his early goal levelled at 1-1 before he sent over a fabulous cross for Keith Houchen's diving header. Born in Manchester on this day, he remains one of the most popular City players of all time.

SATURDAY 11TH JULY 2009

The Sky Blues opened their pre-season campaign with a 1-1 draw against Wrexham at the Racecourse Ground. Jermaine Grandison equalised for City after Marc Williams had opened the scoring for the hosts.

SATURDAY 12TH JULY 2008

The Independent reported that Coventry's pursuit of Wolverhampton Wanderers' striker Freddy Eastwood was close to being finalised after the clubs agreed an undisclosed fee for the player. Chris Coleman had been chasing the Wales international all summer.

FRIDAY 13TH JULY 1979

Craig Bellamy became Coventry's record signing when Gordon Strachan paid Norwich City £6.5 million for him in the summer of 2000. His stay at Highfield Road was brief, just one season, as he departed following relegation. The Sky Blues recouped the fee they paid as Bobby Robson took him to Newcastle United. Born in Cardiff on this day, he played 39 first-team games and scored eight goals.

MONDAY 14TH JULY 2008

Bristol Rovers' manager, Paul Trollope, still hoped to sign Wayne Andrews after the striker's release from Coventry. Trollope spoke to the Bristol Rovers official website when he said: "We have to be careful with him and make sure he's right because he's trying to earn a contract and we are trying to get the best out of him and make sure he's fit enough to secure one." Andrews made 11 substitute appearances for the Sky Blues and famously scored at Barnsley just 26 seconds after entering the field of play in October 2006.

WEDNESDAY 15TH JULY 2009

This Is Nottingham reported Billy Davies' interest in Sky Blues left-back Danny Fox. Fox and Cardiff City's Chris Gunter were Davies' top targets: "There is no doubt about it because we have players in the team who we do not want to fill those positions. We hope to conclude one or two signings over the next few weeks. Time is of the essence over the next week or so."

THURSDAY 16TH JULY 2009

The Sky Blues rejected a £2 million bid from Nottingham Forest for Danny Fox.

TUESDAY 17TH JULY 2007

Speaking to the *Coventry Evening Telegraph*, new signing Ellery Cairo believed his style of play would suit the Championship: "I don't know too much about the Championship but people tell me it is harder than the Premiership because they are all fighting to get up, so I just have to see what happens. Right winger is my position and if they need one I am here – they have got one."

TUESDAY 18TH JULY 1967

Following Coventry's promotion to Division One, the forthcoming season's fixtures were announced. Their first game in the top flight would see them travel to Burnley, followed three days later by a visit to the City Ground. Highfield Road would welcome Sheffield United for its inaugural Division One match before bizarrely playing Nottingham Forest again, just seven days after the away clash. There was a treat in store on Boxing Day as Liverpool would visit while the season closed with a visit to The Dell.

THURSDAY 18TH JULY 1968

Signed by his father, Bobby, Jonathan Gould joined Coventry at the beginning of the Premier League. Between August 1992 and his departure for Bradford City in early 1996 he made 27 first-team appearances for the club. His Sky Blues debut came in the 5-1 win over Liverpool at Highfield Road in December 1992, followed by the 3-0 Boxing Day win over Aston Villa. Born in Paddington, he later spent six seasons as Celtic's number one and played twice for Scotland.

THURSDAY 19TH JULY 2007

Iain Dowie was pleased with the Sky Blues' performance in the 2-2 draw at Shrewsbury Town. Speaking to the *Coventry Evening Telegraph* he said: "Two goals were very good and Ellery had an outstanding debut and Stuart Giddings was back in there and that was probably the most crosses we've got in a long time. And Gids scoring – a full-back in the box – that is something we've worked on because we feel we didn't get enough goals last year. So there were some good things but I expected their legs to be heavy because they have been working tremendously hard and it was nice not to lose."

SATURDAY 19TH JULY 2008

Former Sky Blue Dean Holdsworth, manager of Newport County, signed another former City player, Paul Hall, for his assault on the Conference South title. Hall made 13 first-team appearances over two seasons and scored the winner in a Worthington Cup win over Southend United in September 1998. Signed by Gordon Strachan for £300,000 he moved to Walsall when his contract expired.

MONDAY 20TH JULY 1936

John Sillett, along with George Curtis, took over when Don Mackay resigned in April 1986. Just 13 months later the pair brought unprecedented joy and happiness to Coventry City supporters worldwide by lifting the FA Cup at Wembley. Before taking sole charge in May 1987 and being replaced by Terry Butcher in November 1990, no relegation battles ensued as City established themselves as a 'top half' side amongst the elite. Born in Normansland, Hampshire on this day, Sillett the right-back played his part in the Division Three promotion in 1963/64. The Sutton United and Northampton Town cup defeats were major shocks but 23 years after the cup success his popularity amongst City supporters affords him legend status. Instrumental in revitalising the career of Cyrille Regis, the attacking football preached by 'Snoz' made Coventry an entertaining side to watch in the late 1980s.

MONDAY 21ST JULY 1947

Ray Graydon, who made his Coventry debut in a 3-1 win over Derby County at Highfield Road in August 1977, was born in Bristol. Signed from Aston Villa by Gordon Milne, Graydon provided the ammunition for Ian Wallace and Mick Ferguson from the right wing as City finished seventh in Division One, scoring 75 goals. Graydon made 24 first-team appearances and scored six goals, famously remembered for the fifth and winning goal in the 5-4 win over Norwich City. He left City in the summer of 1978 to join Washington Diplomats in the North American Soccer League.

SATURDAY 21ST JULY 1979

Born in Leuven, Belgium, Laurent Delorge made his Coventry debut at Bramall Lane in a 1-0 win over Sheffield United in September 2001. Within a minute of his introduction he slid home the winner with his first touch of the ball. Signed by Gordon Strachan from AA Gent in season 1998/99, Delorge failed to make an appearance in the three years before City tumbled into Division One. He departed for Lierse SK, released by Gary McAllister, after 34 first-team games which brought four goals. Delorge joined City as a 19-year-old on a five-year contract during the Premiership tenure and is now with Dutch side Roda JC after a brief spell with Ajax.

TUESDAY 21st JULY 1992

Coventry signed Phil Babb from Bradford City for £500,000 under the management of Bobby Gould. He would make his debut on the opening day of the new FA Premier League as substitute in the 2-1 win over Middlesbrough at Highfield Road. In the Coca Cola Cup second-round tie at home to Scarborough, Babb made his first full appearance as a centre-forward.

SUNDAY 22nd JULY 1928

Jimmy Hill OBE was born on this day in Balham, south London. After a playing career with Brentford and Fulham, he retired as a player at the age of 33 and was appointed Coventry manager by chairman Derrick Robins in November 1961. As the Sky Blue revolution began in earnest, Hill changed the playing kit to sky blue, coining the nickname 'The Sky Blues'. He penned the club song and introduced the Sky Blue special trains to away games. The Division Three and Two championships were secured before he departed to take up a position with London Weekend Television as the top-flight tenure was about to begin. In 1975 he returned to the club as managing director and subsequently chairman in 1980 when he introduced the first-ever all-seater stadium to Highfield Road. It is fair to say when the curtain came down on Highfield Road the ovation afforded to Jimmy Hill as he walked out on to the pitch that day will never be matched.

MONDAY 23rd JULY 2007

New signing Leon Best was looking forward to the start of the new season. Speaking to the *Coventry Evening Telegraph* he said: "There was a good deal – all respect to Southampton – on the table but Iain Dowie persuaded me to come here and I have wanted to play under him for a long time because I have heard wonderful things about him. I had a few options in League One but I thought the best thing for me would be to test myself in the Championship. I am enjoying it so far even though the training is really hard. It is definitely the hardest pre-season I have done but the balls have been out since day one which is always good mentally, because you are not just seeing tracks and running."

FRIDAY 24TH JULY 2009

Chris Coleman signed Sammy Clingan for the Sky Blues on a three-year contract for an undisclosed fee after his relegation with Norwich City. The signing of the Northern Ireland international allowed the Coventry manager to release Michael Doyle to Leeds United on a season-long loan deal.

MONDAY 25TH JULY 1960

Signed by John Sillett and George Curtis from Scunthorpe United in the summer of 1986, Coventry City's very own 'Roy of the Rovers', Keith Houchen was born in Middlesbrough. His debut came at Upton Park as West Ham United won 1-0 in August 1986. During the famous 1986/87 season, Houchen played 20 league games with a return of just two goals. In the FA Cup he scored five in five including the fabulous diving header in the final which also provided him with the Goal of the Season. Following his departure to Hibernian in 1991, he had made a total of 66 first-team appearances and scored 12 goals for Coventry. In 2009 he appeared on Sky Sports' *Time of Their Lives* alongside Brian Kilcline and Dave Bennett to talk about the famous cup run. A hero to Coventry supporters, his diving header was one of the very best.

FRIDAY 26TH JULY 1996

Gary McAllister signed for Coventry from Leeds United for a club record £3 million. The shock move united the Scottish international with former teammate Gordon Strachan. Speaking to the *Daily Mirror*, McAllister said: "It was a big decision to leave Leeds. But the board here have shown just as much ambition and commitment as the new board are promising to do at Elland Road. They were the team who came up with the fee and the financial package. It appealed to me to work with Ron Atkinson, and particularly with Gordon Strachan, again. Gordon is perhaps the biggest influence in my decision to come here. His enthusiasm is second to none. If it doesn't rub off on you, then you have a problem as a professional footballer. I won't be making any wild claims about us winning the Premiership – we are still a bit behind Manchester United! – but if your ideal is only to survive then that is all you will do."

MONDAY 27TH JULY 2009

Former Sky Blues manager Micky Adams issued Kevin Thornton with an ultimatum as he joined Port Vale on trial following the cancellation of his Coventry contract. Speaking to *The Sentinel*, Adams said: "Kevin Thornton is a player I know well. He has tremendous ability, I thought we saw that at times, but he's not fit."

WEDNESDAY 28TH JULY 1920

At a public meeting at the Corn Exchange, the Coventry City Supporters' Club officially formed. The group would raise large amounts of money for major ground improvements as well as volunteering their services for any work that would help the club.

MONDAY 29TH JULY 1963

David Phillips, who joined the Sky Blues from Manchester City in the summer of 1986, was born in Wegberg, Germany. During three seasons with the club he made 123 first-team appearances and scored 11 goals. Having reached the FA Cup semi-finals with Plymouth Argyle in 1984, he went one better with the Sky Blues in 1987, his performance at right-back nullifying the threat of Steve Hodge. Norwich City broke their transfer record when they signed him for £550,000 in the summer of 1989.

THURSDAY 30TH JULY 2009

Paul Sullivan, a member of Marcus Hall's testimonial committee, urged supporters to turn out in numbers for the match against Everton on Sunday. Speaking to the *Coventry Evening Telegraph* he said: "We want this to be a great day for Marcus and hope that City fans come out in force to get behind him and the Sky Blues in their last big match before the start of the new season."

MONDAY 31ST JULY 2000

After just under one season at Highfield Road, Robbie Keane transferred to Inter Milan for £13 million, a record sale for the Sky Blues and a profit of £7 million. Gordon Strachan told the *Daily Mirror*: "I shall be desperately sorry to see Robbie go because you aren't given the opportunity to work with that sort of talent very often. Robbie is something very special, I believe he deserves the description 'great'."

COVENTRY CITY
On This Day

AUGUST

SATURDAY 1st AUGUST 1987

Around 51,000 Sky Blues supporters made the trip to Wembley to participate in the season's annual opener, the Charity Shield. League champions Everton were the opponents as Wayne Clarke's 44th-minute goal took the trophy to Merseyside. New signing David Speedie lined up alongside Keith Houchen and there were substitute appearances for Steve Sedgley and Brian Borrows, who both missed out the previous May.

MONDAY 2nd AUGUST 1943

Jimmy Hill paid a world-record fee for a goalkeeper when he signed Bill Glazier from Crystal Palace for £35,000. Glazier would spend ten seasons as the City number one and made 395 first-team appearances between 1964 and 1974. His final game at Highfield Road in November 1974 brought an outstanding performance in a 1-1 draw with Liverpool. Born in Nottingham on this day, Glazier won three England under-23 caps while at City and ended his career at Brentford before retiring shortly afterwards.

SUNDAY 2nd AUGUST 2009

Coventry drew 2-2 with Premier League side Everton in the testimonial game for long-serving left-back Marcus Hall. Tim Cahill opened the scoring before Michael Doyle levelled. Young Everton substitute Jose Baxter restored Everton's lead until Aron Gunnarsson completed the scoring. Just over 8,000 supporters attended for local lad Hall's big day.

MONDAY 3rd AUGUST 2009

Coventry manager Chris Coleman was hopeful of signing Bristol City winger Michael McIndoe before the opening game at home to Ipswich Town. Speaking to Sky Sports, Coleman said: "I know that it has come out that we have agreed a fee with Bristol City, but we are yet to agree other things so the deal is far from being done. I am hoping, praying and fingers are crossed because we owe it to the supporters and the boys we have got who have done a great job over the last six weeks. They have got their heads down and got on with it. Last year they had all the speculation that we were signing this one and signing that one and this year they have just got on with it."

SATURDAY 4TH AUGUST 1956

For the first time ever, the Sky Blues signed a player from the New York Cosmos. Having lined up alongside the great Pele and Franz Beckenbauer, Steve Hunt joined Coventry in September 1978 and made a goalscoring debut in a 2-0 win at Highfield Road against Derby County. He possessed one of the best left foots the ground had ever seen and made 216 first-team appearances until his departure to West Bromwich Albion in March 1984. Born in Witton, Birmingham, 34 goals were added over his six seasons in sky blue.

SUNDAY 4TH AUGUST 1963

Born in South Shields, Don Mackay signed left-sided midfielder Nick Pickering from Sunderland in February 1986. One of City's cup-winning heroes, Pickering made 94 first-team appearances and scored ten goals raiding down the Sky Blues' left wing. Following the impact of David Smith's introduction to the first team, he moved to left-back at the end of season 1987/88 before moving to Derby County in the summer of 1988. He retired in 1994 after failing to recover from a foot injury.

WEDNESDAY 5TH AUGUST 2009

Long-serving midfielder Michael Doyle was poised to move to Leeds United on a season-long loan deal following the signing of Sammy Clingan.

WEDNESDAY 6TH AUGUST 1975

Willie Boland came through the youth system and made his debut as substitute in a 2-1 defeat to Chelsea at Stamford Bridge. Over the course of the next six seasons, Boland, who was born in Ennis, Republic of Ireland, made 72 first-team appearances and failed to score during this time. His contract expired in the summer of 1999 and a move to Cardiff City saw him make over 200 first-team appearances over the following four seasons. Boland moved on to Hartlepool United and retired from football in September 2009 having failed to overcome knee injuries. Speaking to the club website he said: "I've got used to not playing. I wouldn't be able to do myself justice."

FRIDAY 7TH AUGUST 1998

Fresh from the Croatian national side's third-place finish in the 1998 World Cup finals, Gordon Strachan brought in Robert Jarni, their attack-minded left-back, for £2.6 million. There were high hopes for Jarni as City had finished an encouraging 11th the previous May. With just eight days until the opening game at Highfield Road against Chelsea the expectations had been raised a few notches by the signing.

THURSDAY 7TH AUGUST 2008

Chris Coleman signed Clinton Morrison on a two-year deal following the expiry of his Crystal Palace contract. The 29-year-old trained with the squad throughout pre-season and was delighted to finally sign. Speaking to the official club website he said: "I'm delighted to have finally got a deal done. Me and Leon McKenzie were strike partners at Palace and he's been calling me all the time telling me I should sign and I'm really pleased. I can score goals at this level and now I'm looking forward to doing that for Coventry so I'm hoping I can play some part against Norwich on Saturday."

SATURDAY 8TH AUGUST 1981

Signed by Gary McAllister from Celtic in the summer of 2003, Michael Doyle was born on this day. Player of the Year in 2004/05, Doyle, who was born in Dublin, and had made 279 first-team appearances and scored 21 goals up to the end of 2009/10.

SATURDAY 9TH AUGUST 2003

While making their way to Vicarage Road for the season's opener at Watford, City's 3,000-strong following were stunned to hear the game had been cancelled. Signed on a season's loan from Manchester United, Watford winger Jimmy Davis had died in a car crash earlier that morning and Watford called the game off shortly after midday. Sir Alex Ferguson, speaking to the BBC Sport website said: "You could not meet a nicer and more bubbly character than Jimmy Davis. He was a player with real potential, that's why we sent him to Watford this season. At 21 he had great promise. We are all really sad. It's terrible news."

SATURDAY 10TH AUGUST 2002

Gary McAllister's first game as Coventry player-manager welcomed Sheffield United to Highfield Road. New signings Morten Hyldgaard and Dean Gordon lined up in front of 18,837 as the Sky Blues came from behind to cancel out Carl Asaba's fantastic strike. Jay Bothroyd and Gary McSheffrey sent the city masses home happy with the three points as McAllister started his managerial career with a victory.

FRIDAY 11TH AUGUST 1989

Sky Blues' reserve goalkeeper Jake Findlay prepared for his testimonial game the following day against West Bromwich Albion. It was unique for the fact that Findlay had not made a single first-team appearance for Coventry but had been forced to retire through injury. His big day saw 3,596 supporters turn out to watch a sparkling performance from new signing Dougie McGuire, a right winger brought in from Celtic. Colin West's goal gave Albion a 1-0 win.

SATURDAY 12TH AUGUST 1961

Peter Bodak, who made his Coventry debut in a 3-1 win over Crystal Palace at Highfield Road in September 1980, was born in Birmingham. Over the next two seasons he played 44 times and scored seven goals before he transferred to Manchester City in the spring of 1982.

TUESDAY 12TH AUGUST 1969

Willie Carr scored a first-half hat-trick as the Sky Blues swept aside West Bromwich Albion 3-1 at Highfield Road. Albion's debutant goalkeeper Gordon Nisbet would change position in later years and ended up as a solid and reliable right-back with over 600 first-team appearances to his name. Bobby Gould made his Sky Blues debut in the number seven shirt as over 37,000 watched Coventry beat a West Bromwich side which contained Jeff Astle.

SATURDAY 12TH AUGUST 1972

Gordon Milne and Joe Mercer replaced caretaker manager Bob Dennison during the summer of 1972. Their first game in charge saw City travel to White Hart Lane where two goals from Martin Peters gave the hosts a 2-1 win. Ernie Hunt had levelled on 62 minutes in front of 33,884 supporters.

FRIDAY 13TH AUGUST 1883

The greatest football club in the world was founded on this day as Singers FC. The bulk of the club's players came from the Singer Cycle Factory and the club was formed by William Stanley who became the first manager. Singers changed their name to Coventry City Football Club in 1898.

SATURDAY 14TH AUGUST 1993

A sensational 3-0 win at Highbury brought last season's FA Cup winners back down to earth with a bump. Mick Quinn scored the club's first Premier League hat-trick as David Seaman and 24,897 watched in horror as the Sky Blues played the Gunners off the pitch. George Graham, speaking to the *Daily Mirror* after the game said: "I warned my players Coventry always start the season well, but they didn't respond. They had a lot more desire than us and we seemed to forget that English football is as much about application and drive as it is about ability." Quinn left clutching the matchball, annoyed he missed a chance for a late fourth: "I should have scored. It was a case of tiredness and cockiness. I don't normally bet on football, but I've had £50 on myself to finish top scorer and now my odds will probably fall."

SATURDAY 15TH AUGUST 1992

Bobby Gould began his second spell as Coventry manager with a 2-1 win at Highfield Road against Middlesbrough. The game also marked the beginning of the Premier League and new signing John Williams, nicknamed the 'flying postman', scored the opening goal after just nine minutes. He was beaten to the title of first-ever Premier League goal by Sheffield United's Brian Deane who headed past Peter Schmeichel after just five minutes.

SATURDAY 16TH AUGUST 1980

Newly promoted Birmingham City won 3-1 in the season's opener in front of 21,907 at St. Andrew's. Alan Curbishley (two) and Kevin Dillon opened up a 3-0 lead before Andy Blair added a late consolation. The Sky Blues' task was made even harder by Ray Gooding's dismissal for punching Archie Gemmill just after half-time.

THURSDAY 17TH AUGUST 1967

Having led the Sky Blues to two championships, manager Jimmy Hill resigned just two days prior to the start of the top-flight sojourn. The 'Head of Sport' role at London Weekend Television was the reason but Hill remained in his post until his successor, Noel Cantwell, was appointed.

THURSDAY 17TH AUGUST 2000

Craig Bellamy joined the Sky Blues for £6.5 million, taking over from Robbie Keane as the club's record signing. The 21-year-old Bellamy joined from Norwich City and manager Gordon Strachan was praised by chairman Bryan Richardson for yet another coup. Speaking to the *Daily Mirror* he said: "Gordon has done the business yet again, convincing Craig that this is the best place for his immediate career. Landing Craig is fantastic for us, especially considering the calibre of the opposition we were up against in attempting to obtain his signature on the vital piece of paper."

SATURDAY 18TH AUGUST 1962

Jimmy Hill introduced a new look all sky blue strip that replaced the all-white affair. With the *Coventry Evening Telegraph* labelling the side 'The Sky Blues', the club had both a new image and nickname. The first outing for the new strip saw Coventry beat Notts County 2-0 at Highfield Road with goals from Terry Bly and Hubert Barr in front of 22,832 fans.

WEDNESDAY 18TH AUGUST 1999

Robbie Keane became the club's new record signing as Gordon Strachan signed him on a five-year contract for £6 million from Wolverhampton Wanderers.

SATURDAY 19TH AUGUST 1961

Michael Gynn, who made 291 first-team appearances and scored 45 goals between 1983 and 1993, was born in Peterborough. Gynn was signed by Bobby Gould for £60,000 and went on to become one of the cup-winning heroes with his wonderful midfield performance at Wembley. On his 31st birthday the Sky Blues won 2-0 at Tottenham Hotspur and the honour of the first-ever Premier League penalty miss went to Gynn.

SATURDAY 19TH AUGUST 1967

The first-ever top flight game for Coventry City resulted in a 2-1 defeat at Burnley. The defeat was the Sky Blues' first since the 3-1 defeat at Huddersfield Town back on November 19th 1966. A Dave Merrington own goal was a consolation strike in front of a huge away following. The match saw the club become the only team to play in all seven divisions of the English league. Bill Glazier, Mick Kearns, Dietmar Bruck, Ron Farmer, George Curtis, Dave Clements, John Key, Ernie Machin, John Tudor, Brian Lewis and Ronnie Rees lined up for City.

SATURDAY 19TH AUGUST 2000

Signed from Liverpool in the close season, David Thompson became the first City debutant to be sent off as Middlesbrough won 3-1 at Highfield Road. Craig Bellamy also made his Coventry debut while City old boy Noel Whelan appeared as a substitute alongside future Sky Blue Keith O'Neill, who completed the 90 minutes. Following this poor start, City would win at Southampton and Manchester City to sit in fourth position but by Christmas they would be entrenched in 18th as relegation loomed.

SUNDAY 19TH AUGUST 2001

Former Coventry goalkeeper Les Sealey sadly died of a heart attack on this day, aged just 43. Born on September 29th 1957 in Bethnal Green, Sealey joined the Sky Blues from school and made his debut at just 17 in a 1-1 draw at Queens Park Rangers. With Jim Blyth his main competition for the number one shirt, there was a fair bit of alternating which maybe explained why neither player played as many games as perhaps their talents permitted. Prior to joining Luton Town in the summer of 1983, Sealey made 180 first-team appearances for the Sky Blues. After Luton, he played for Manchester United, winning the FA Cup and European Cup Winners' Cup, Aston Villa, Blackpool, Leyton Orient and West Ham United. At the time of his death he was coaching the goalkeepers at West Ham and it is often forgotten he came back to City for a two-game loan spell under Don Howe in April 1992 when Steve Ogrizovic was injured.

SATURDAY 20TH AUGUST 1994

Having spent the previous season playing in a three-sided ground, the new East Stand was officially opened for the visit of Wimbledon to Highfield Road. Just 11,005 were in a half-empty stadium as David Busst's second-half header cancelled out Stewart Castledine's low strike. Paul Cook made his City debut as substitute for Leigh Jenkinson while former City striker Mick Harford led the Dons' front line.

THURSDAY 20TH AUGUST 1998

Amazingly, just 13 days after joining Coventry, Robert Jarni moved to Real Madrid for £3.35 million without playing a competitive game for the club. The near profit of £750,000 in just under a fortnight was unbelievable. He would spend just one season with Madrid before moving on to Las Palmas and Panathinaikos.

SATURDAY 20TH AUGUST 2005

The Ricoh Arena opened its doors for the first time to welcome Queens Park Rangers. As a result of the delayed opening, the Sky Blues had played their first three matches away from home with only two points to show. A crowd of 23,043 watched Claus Jorgensen score the first goal at the stadium after ten minutes. Dele Adebola (two) completed the scoring as the visitors' Danny Shittu took the first red card for fouling the Coventry number nine. Former Sky Blue Paul Furlong lined up for Rangers while Willo Flood made his City debut on loan from Manchester City.

FRIDAY 21ST AUGUST 2009

Leon McKenzie was in line to make a comeback after his injury nightmare and earn a new contract as a direct result. A ruptured Achilles against Birmingham City back in February had sidelined the front man but Chris Coleman was eager to get him back to full fitness as he told the club's official website: "I'm hoping to give Leon a little cameo role, perhaps 15-20 minutes. He's not ready for anything more than that but it will be good to see what he can do. We've got him fit, he's been training well but now he needs to get a couple of 90 minutes under his belt. If we think everything's OK we can talk about putting pen to paper."

SATURDAY 22ND AUGUST 1992

Following their opening-day win over Middlesbrough and midweek victory at Tottenham Hotspur, the Sky Blues became the first outright leaders of the newly formed Premier League with a 2-1 win at Wimbledon. Michael Gynn and Robert Rosario sent the side into a 2-0 lead at Selhurst Park before future Sky Blue Dean Holdsworth reduced the deficit in the second half. Three wins out of three kept Coventry in pole position for four days as Queens Park Rangers won with an Andrew Impey goal in the very next match.

TUESDAY 22ND AUGUST 2006

Edgar Street, Hereford, was the scene of yet another cup humiliation. It was the Carling Cup first round with the hosts promoted from the Conference just five months before. Stuart Fleetwood completed his hat-trick by the 64th minute after Dele Adebola had reduced the deficit to 2-1 on the hour. Coventry fielded a strong side but were swept away by Fleetwood who opened the scoring in front of 3,404 after just 48 seconds.

SATURDAY 23RD AUGUST 1958

Following the re-organisation of the Football League structure, the Sky Blues became founder members of the newly formed Division Four. Billy Frith's side began their season with a 0-0 draw against Darlington at Highfield Road. They would spend only one season in the lowest tier as a second-place finish ensured an immediate promotion to Division Three.

FRIDAY 24TH AUGUST 2001

An opening-day win at Stockport County in the first game post relegation raised expectations of an immediate return to the Premier League. Two defeats followed in quick succession as Wolverhampton Wanderers won 1-0 at Highfield Road before the heavily delayed Sky Blues supporters witnessed a 2-1 defeat at Bradford City. Jay Bothroyd scored the consolation after Lee Hughes' straight red card left City with a mountain to climb.

SATURDAY 25TH AUGUST 1984

Steve Ogrizovic, Kirk Stephens, Martin Jol, Brian Kilcline and substitute Kenny Hibbitt all made their debuts in a 1-0 defeat at Aston Villa on the opening day of the season.

SATURDAY 26TH AUGUST 1933

Clarrie Bourton, Jock Lauderdale and Billie Lake all notched doubles as Coventry thrashed Gillingham 7-1 on the opening day of season 1933/34. They would finish the season as runners-up in Division Three (South). This meant no promotion as only the champions received that honour.

SATURDAY 26TH AUGUST 1967

Highfield Road staged top-flight football for the first time. Sheffield United were the visitors as the Sky Blues sought their first win in Division One. Right winger John Key took the accolade of scoring the first top flight goal in a sky blue shirt at the great stadium and was quickly followed by Dietmar Bruck, who completed the scoring to make it 2-2. The 33,328 fans packed into Highfield Road would have to wait another ten days before the first Division One victory was secured. Southampton were beaten 2-1, John Tudor and Ronnie Rees scored the goals.

SATURDAY 27TH AUGUST 1983

Bobby Gould's first spell as Coventry manager began with an away trip to Watford. Debuts were given to Ashley Grimes, Michael Gynn, Dave Bamber, Terry Gibson and substitute Nicky Platnauer. Watford finished the previous season runners-up to Liverpool but City capitalised on own goals from Pat Rice and Ian Bolton, added to by Terry Gibson to win 3-2.

SATURDAY 27TH AUGUST 1988

The opening-day visit to Tottenham Hotspur was called off at 10.30 am on the morning of the game. White Hart Lane failed to land the necessary safety certificate for the new stand and the fixture was prevented from going ahead as planned.

SATURDAY 28TH AUGUST 1982

Perry Suckling was drafted in by Dave Sexton for his Coventry debut at Highfield Road against Southampton. With Les Sealey injured, Suckling kept a clean sheet as Steve Whitton fired past Peter Shilton to give the Sky Blues a 1-0 win. Aged 16 years and 320 days, he became Highfield Road's youngest-ever debutant and would make four appearances during the season including the 2-1 shocker at home to Burnley in the League Cup.

SATURDAY 29TH AUGUST 1981

Dave Sexton's first game as Coventry manager welcomed Ron Atkinson's Manchester United to a sold-out Highfield Road. The match was significant for being the first game in the new all-seater stadium, the first of its kind. Goals from Steve Whitton and Peter Bodak sandwiched a Lou Macari strike to give the Sky Blues three points for a win for the very first time.

SATURDAY 30TH AUGUST 1919

Coventry made their Football League debut as Tottenham Hotspur were the visitors to Highfield Road. In front of just over 16,000 supporters, the London side won 5-0 and City would finish the season in 20th position, just safe from relegation.

SATURDAY 30TH AUGUST 1980

Clive Hayward made his only first-team appearance in a 1-0 defeat at Villa Park, wearing the number seven shirt. Born on November 1st 1960 in Ramsgate, Hayward came through the ranks at City and was sold in 1981 to Washington Diplomats in the North American Soccer League. He retired aged 27 in 1987 following a spell in Hong Kong.

WEDNESDAY 30TH AUGUST 1989

Goals from Michael Gynn and David Smith gave the Sky Blues a 2-1 victory over Manchester City at Highfield Road. The result took City top of Division One for the first time ever; a 4-1 defeat at Millwall awaited the new leaders just ten days later.

FRIDAY 31ST AUGUST 1973

Gordon Strachan signed attacking right-back Regis Genaux in the summer of 1996. Genaux – who would make just four first-team appearances before leaving six months later to join Udinese – was born in Charleroi, Belgium. He retired at the age of 29 and sadly died of heart failure in November 2008 aged just 35.

TUESDAY 31ST AUGUST 1976

The team coach broke down on the way home from Ashton Gate following the Sky Blues' League Cup win at Bristol City. Mick Ferguson scored the winning goal in the 41st minute.

COVENTRY CITY
On This Day

SEPTEMBER

SATURDAY 1st SEPTEMBER 1962

Club record-signing Terry Bly scored a hat-trick as Southend United visited Highfield Road and took the points with a 4-3 victory. Bly would stay just one season, scoring 26 league goals in 32 games before he was replaced in early April by new £21,000 record-signing George Hudson, also captured from Peterborough United. Promotion would have to wait until April 1964 as Jimmy Hill pushed on for the top flight.

SATURDAY 1st SEPTEMBER 1979

Prior to the home match against Norwich City, Jim Blyth injured his back in the warm-up and was unable to continue. Youth team goalkeeper Steve Murcott had already played in the morning and was summoned to the dressing room to take Blyth's place. In his only City appearance, the 18-year-old kept a clean sheet as the Sky Blues won 2-0 with goals from Bobby McDonald and Mick Ferguson.

SATURDAY 1st SEPTEMBER 1984

Bobby Gould appealed for calm over the public address system as Sky Blues and Leicester City supporters clashed on the pitch shortly after kick off. Ten minutes later referee Tony Ward brought the teams back onto the field and Coventry completed a 2-0 win with goals from Bob Latchford and Dave Bennett. Future Sky Blue, Kevin MacDonald, left the field injured for the Foxes prior to his departure to Liverpool.

SATURDAY 1st SEPTEMBER 1990

Four penalties were awarded by referee David Axcell as City and Nottingham Forest shared a 2-2 draw at Highfield Road. Brian Kilcline scored and missed one before Brian Borrows took over to level with two minutes remaining. Nigel Jemson scored both of the visitors' goals, the first from the spot.

SATURDAY 2nd SEPTEMBER 1967

Fresh from promotion to the top flight, the Sky Blue Army headed to Highbury for the first time. A crowd of 30,404 witnessed Bobby Gould open the scoring before George Graham levelled with 11 minutes remaining.

WEDNESDAY 2ND SEPTEMBER 1992

Another win on the road at Hillsborough made it three wins out of three away from Highfield Road. Peter Ndlovu opened the scoring before Lee Hurst made it two shortly after half-time. Chris Bart-Williams gave the hosts hope but City held on for the three points which took them up to second position.

SATURDAY 3RD SEPTEMBER 1977

Leeds United roared into a two-goal lead after just 17 minutes at Highfield Road. Ray Hankin and Gordon McQueen gave the Sky Blues a mountain to climb in front of 21,312 supporters. Strike pairing Mick Ferguson and Ian Wallace rescued Coventry with goals either side of half-time to take the side up to eighth in Division One.

THURSDAY 4TH SEPTEMBER 1941

Former club physiotherapist George Dalton joined the Sky Blues upon Norman Pilgrim's departure in 1976. Born in Dilston, he treated David Busst's horrific leg fractures at Old Trafford and sat alongside George and John on that wonderful day at Wembley.

SATURDAY 4TH SEPTEMBER 1965

Following the introduction of the single substitute rule brought in for injuries only, Coventry had to wait for their fifth league game to utilise the option for the first time. Left-back Dietmar Bruck replaced the injured Ron Farmer at half-time during the 3-3 draw with Manchester City at Highfield Road.

SATURDAY 4TH SEPTEMBER 1971

City and Chelsea shared a six-goal thriller at Stamford Bridge as all the goals came before half-time. Billy Rafferty, John O'Rourke and Dennis Mortimer scored for the Sky Blues, Chelsea replied through Peter Osgood (two) and John Hollins.

SATURDAY 4TH SEPTEMBER 1976

Bobby McDonald and Terry Yorath made their debuts in a 3-1 defeat away to Liverpool. Mick Ferguson scored within the first minute before the reigning champions hit back with goals from Kevin Keegan, David Johnson and John Toshack.

MONDAY 5TH SEPTEMBER 1960

Billy Frith's side shared eight goals with Queens Park Rangers at Highfield Road. Ray Straw scored twice, Ron Farmer once, and a penalty from Bill Myerscough made it 4-4 in front of just under 16,000 supporters.

SATURDAY 6TH SEPTEMBER 1980

Match of the Day cameras visited Highfield Road for the visit of Crystal Palace. After a goalless first half Gerry Daly scored two goals in four minutes after Clive Allen had given Palace a 47th-minute lead. Shortly afterwards, Allen fired a shot past Jim Blyth which smashed into the goal net stanchion and bounced back into play. As Allen celebrated, the linesman was consulted and play waved on as furious Palace players chased after the referee. To add insult to injury, Andy Blair scored a third for City in a game which saw Peter Bodak make his Coventry debut.

TUESDAY 6TH SEPTEMBER 1983

Coventry fought back from conceding Justin Fashanu's early goal to win 2-1 at Highfield Road against Notts County. Terry Gibson and Nicky Platnauer took the three points for the Sky Blues in front of 11,016 fans. Wembley cup-winning captain Brian Kilcline lined up for the visitors alongside Nigel Worthington and Martin O'Neill. County ended the season in the bottom three and Kilcline moved on to the West Midlands.

SATURDAY 7TH SEPTEMBER 1935

The 1935/36 season would see the Bantams crowned Division Three (South) champions. Their first win had to wait until the third game when Newport County were the visitors. Clarrie Bourton scored a hattrick with further goals from Leslie Jones (two) and Jock Lauderdale (two) as Coventry won 7-1.

SATURDAY 7TH SEPTEMBER 1991

Arsenal right-back Lee Dixon gifted City the lead after just 56 seconds with a 30-yard chip over his own goalkeeper, David Seaman. Just four months earlier the Gunners had thrashed City 6-1 as they sealed the title. Peter Ndlovu added a late second goal before Tony Adams' consolation.

SATURDAY 8TH SEPTEMBER 2001

Grimsby Town inflicted a 1-0 defeat on the Sky Blues in what would prove to be Gordon Strachan's final match in charge. Three defeats out of the first five matches post relegation led to loud protests from the supporters against Strachan and chairman Bryan Richardson. Phil Jevons scored the only goal of the game when he punished a Magnus Hedman error in front of just under 15,000 fans.

SATURDAY 9TH SEPTEMBER 1899

Highfield Road staged its first competitive Birmingham & District League match with the visit of Shrewsbury Town. A 1-0 win for the club was watched by 3,000 supporters at the beginning of a season where they would finish in 16th position.

SATURDAY 9TH SEPTEMBER 1989

Having sat in top spot for ten days, the Sky Blues were unceremoniously dumped off their perch by the 'Lions' of Millwall. Teddy Sheringham scored within the first minute on a rain-sodden day in Bermondsey. A further Teddy strike, along with one by Steve Anthrobus, gave Millwall a 3-0 half-time lead. To make matters worse, Steve Ogrizovic only played the first 45 minutes after succumbing to injury, his place for the second half taken by David Speedie. David Smith gave Coventry hope but left-back Ian Dawes finally beat Speedie in the final minute to wrap up a 4-1 win. Ogrizovic would miss the following game at home to Luton Town due to the shoulder injury sustained at The Den. The win took Millwall top of Division One but a poor run over the winter months would see them relegated, finishing bottom of the league.

FRIDAY 9TH SEPTEMBER 1994

Phil Neal signed Dion Dublin from Manchester United for a fee of £2 million. This was generated by the sale of Phil Babb to Liverpool days previously for a new record fee for a defender – £3.75 million. Dublin went straight into the side for the next day's game at Loftus Road, where he scored the equaliser with six minutes remaining. Gary Penrice scored both Queens Park Rangers goals after Paul Cook had opened the scoring.

THURSDAY 10TH SEPTEMBER 1970

Twins Craig and Lee Middleton were born on this day in Nuneaton. Craig scored in the first leg of the victorious FA Youth Cup final in 1987 against Charlton Athletic while brother Lee played right-back in both games as the Sky Blues won 2-1 on aggregate. Craig made his debut as substitute for Michael Gynn in Coventry's 3-2 defeat at White Hart Lane in April 1990. He went on to make four first-team appearances before a move to Cambridge United in the summer of 1993. Following his stay at Cambridge he also played for Cardiff City and Halifax Town. Lee made just two substitute appearances. His debut came at Stamford Bridge as he replaced Dean Emerson in City's 1-0 defeat. In the summer of 1990 he was released and moved into non-league football with Corby Town.

SATURDAY 10TH SEPTEMBER 1983

West Ham United's Ray Stewart missed only five penalties during 11 years with the Hammers. One of those was saved by City's Perry Suckling prior to a 5-2 defeat at Upton Park. Trevor Peake and Nicky Platnauer fired the Sky Blues into a two-goal lead after 15 minutes. West Ham hit back through a David Swindlehurst hat-trick and a double from recently transferred former Sky Blue, Steve Whitton, who fired in one of his trademark thunderbolts.

WEDNESDAY 11TH SEPTEMBER 1968

Ron Atkinson signed Richard Shaw from Crystal Palace in November 1995 for £1 million. Over the next 11 seasons, he made 338 first-team appearances, and is currently tenth in the all-time appearance list. Born in Brentford on this day, Shaw scored just once in a sky blue shirt, a right-footed rocket in the 5-2 win at Gillingham in May 2004. He was rewarded for his loyalty with a testimonial against Celtic at the Ricoh Arena. Around 25,000 fans walked through the turnstiles as City won 3-1 and Shaw was delighted with the turnout as he spoke to the BBC Sport website: "To get over 25,000 is amazing and I'm very touched. They (the Celtic fans) were fantastic and never stopped singing but I'd also like to pay tribute to our fans as well because they turned out in their thousands and showed their appreciation for the ten years I've been here."

THURSDAY 12TH SEPTEMBER 1957

Steve Ogrizovic, Coventry City's leading appearance maker with an impressive record of 601 first-team games (and one goal), was born in Mansfield. Signed from Shrewsbury Town for £72,500 in the summer of 1984, he previously understudied Ray Clemence and Bruce Grobbelaar at Liverpool. He played league football through the 1970s, 1980s, 1990s and into the new millennium; he was selected to represent the Football League against the Rest of the World at Wembley in 1987. His 601st and final appearance, against Sheffield Wednesday at Highfield Road, ended with a lap of honour and thunderous applause from the City faithful. Just 13 months later the Sky Blues were relegated to the second tier. Following retirement he remains at the club as reserve team coach, combining his duties with coaching the City goalkeepers.

SATURDAY 12TH SEPTEMBER 1981

With their team in decline and relegation a reality the following May, Leeds United supporters rioted during their 4-0 defeat at Highfield Road. Seats were ripped up and rained down on both rival supporters in the Sky Blue Stand and the players on the pitch. Rudi Kaiser, Steve Whitton and two from Garry Thompson took Coventry up to eighth position in Division One. With Highfield Road newly converted into an all-seater stadium, Jimmy Hill's claim that "you can't be a hooligan sitting down" seemed to hold little credence.

SATURDAY 13TH SEPTEMBER 1969

Neil Martin scored two second-half penalties as City retrieved a half-time deficit to share the points with Crystal Palace at Highfield Road. A 29,310 crowd watched the Sky Blues fight back as they dropped a place to seventh in the table with the 2-2 draw.

SATURDAY 13TH SEPTEMBER 1980

Peter Bodak's third-minute goal gave City the points at Molineux as the hosts paraded their new stand which would nearly bankrupt the club. Only 18,115 watched the Sky Blues' first away win of the season as Steve Jacobs made his Coventry debut. Wolves' side included Andy Gray and former Sky Blue Willie Carr.

SATURDAY 14TH SEPTEMBER 1968

City played out a goalless draw with Nottingham Forest at Meadow Lane, home of neighbours Notts County. A fire ensured that the City Ground could not host football for a short while so just over 22,000 supporters did not have far to travel to witness two sides who would finish just above the relegation zone.

MONDAY 14TH SEPTEMBER 1992

Sky brought its 'Monday Night Football' concept to Highfield Road for the first time. The fireworks extravaganza, hosted by Sky Blues supporter Richard Keys, welcomed Tottenham Hotspur and the crowd of 15,293 was probably lower as a result of the game being televised around pubs and living rooms across the city. John Williams scored the solitary goal after 61 minutes, beating Ian Walker in the Londoners' goal.

TUESDAY 14TH SEPTEMBER 1999

The first leg of the Worthington Cup tie against Tranmere Rovers left the Sky Blues with a mountain to climb for the return. Goalkeeper Raffaele Nuzzo made his only Coventry appearance and picked the ball out of the net on five occasions. Gary McAllister gave City a seventh-minute lead which lasted until just after half-time. A double from Scott Taylor and a hat-trick from much travelled David Kelly gave the Merseyside club a 5-1 home win as a strong City side succumbed under pressure. A rescue act was on the cards in the return leg but Tranmere went through 6-4 on aggregate.

SATURDAY 15TH SEPTEMBER 1945

Dave Clements, who was signed as an 18-year-old by Jimmy Hill from Wolverhampton Wanderers, was born in Larne, Northern Ireland. Signed in 1964, Clements made 257 first-team appearances before his departure to Sheffield Wednesday in 1971. He scored 30 goals during his time at Highfield Road and gained 21 Northern Ireland caps, at the time a club record. He went on to play for Everton and combined this with a player-manager role for the national side before moving to the USA in 1976 for a cameo with the New York Cosmos where he played alongside Pele.

WEDNESDAY 16TH SEPTEMBER 1970

Following the sixth-place finish at the end of season 1969/70, Noel Cantwell led his City side into Europe, more specifically, Bulgaria. Trakia Plovdiv were the European Fairs Cup first-round opponents for the Sky Blues and City travelled for the first leg which they won in spectacular fashion, 4-1. John O'Rourke scored a hat-trick, assisted by a strike from Neil Martin. The side that night comprised: Bill Glazier, Mick Coop, Wilf Smith, Ernie Machin, Jeff Blockley, Geoff Strong, Ernie Hunt, Willie Carr, Neil Martin, John O'Rourke and Dave Clements. The Fairs Cup would be renamed the European Cup Winners' Cup in years to come. English teams were banned from competing in Europe following the Heysel tragedy and this prevented the 1987 side from participating in the same competition.

TUESDAY 16TH SEPTEMBER 1997

On a night of driving rain and wind along the Golden Mile, Coventry travelled to Blackpool for the first round, first leg of the Coca Cola Cup. Ferocious rains drenched City supporters standing on the open Kop area and pedantic stewarding prevented them from joining the rest of the City faithful sheltering in the stand. David Linighan headed home the winner for third tier Blackpool who took the slender advantage into the second leg. Following the game, Sky Blues' striker Kyle Lightbourne complained that when he ran clear on goal in the first half, a laser pen was shone in his eyes by a home supporter sat behind the goal. Speaking to the *Coventry Evening Telegraph* he said: "It's dangerous and should not be allowed. I just turned around and it caught me right in the eye." Inspector Tony Pinder of Blackpool police said: "We know they're being used, but it is hard to pin down who is pointing them."

THURSDAY 17TH SEPTEMBER 1970

Manager Noel Cantwell praised the excellent performance in Bulgaria. Speaking to the *Daily Mirror* he said: "It was a great performance. I was delighted with the way the lads played, considering this is their first experience of the Fairs Cup." Chairman Derrick Robins said: "People at home will think it was easy. But it wasn't. They could have murdered us in the first 20 minutes until we started scoring."

SATURDAY 18TH SEPTEMBER 1982

Derek Hall made his only Coventry first-team appearance in a 1-0 defeat to Birmingham City at St. Andrew's. A central midfielder, Hall made his debut alongside fellow new boys Keith Thompson and Jim Melrose. Having joined the club as an apprentice he moved on to Torquay United in the summer of 1984 and enjoyed successful lower division spells with Swindon Town, Southend United, Halifax Town, Hereford United and Rochdale before moving into non-league football. As of 2009, Hall had moved into coaching and was living in South Australia.

SATURDAY 19TH SEPTEMBER 1942

October 1969 saw centre-half Roy Barry join the Sky Blues from Dunfermline Athletic. Barry, who made his debut as substitute in a 1-0 defeat at Stamford Bridge, was born in Edinburgh. He replaced George Curtis in City's back four as they went on to secure sixth place and European football. In March 1970, he broke his leg in a 1-1 draw with Sheffield Wednesday at Highfield Road and would not return until the final game of season 1970/71, 14 months later. In the summer of 1973, Crystal Palace signed him after making 97 first-team appearances and scoring two goals for the Sky Blues. During the 1982 FA Cup run, that took the Sky Blues to the quarter-finals, they defeated Oxford United 4-0 in the fifth round. Caretaker manager for Oxford that day was Roy Barry who kept the seat warm for future Coventry assistant manager Jim Smith.

SATURDAY 19TH SEPTEMBER 1998

Newcastle United visited Highfield Road and took all three points with a superb display of finishing. Noel Whelan opened the scoring after just five minutes but by half-time the Sky Blues were 3-1 down, goals from Nikos Dabizas, Alan Shearer and Gary Speed. Stephen Glass and Shearer made the final score 5-1 and a baptism of fire for new Sky Blues centre-half Jean Guy Wallemme, who signed in the summer. Wallemme joined from Racing Club Lens in France's First Division and made just eight first-team appearances before returning home to Sochaux in December. The defeat left City in 19th position; they failed to make it into the top half of the table all season and finished in 15th.

SATURDAY 20TH SEPTEMBER 1969

City visited Maine Road to take on Malcolm Allison's all stars but were under pressure from the kick off as Colin Bell scored within the first minute. Francis Lee added a penalty before Ernie Hunt gave the Sky Blues hope of a point. Late pressure saw the hosts break and seal a 3-1 victory with a second goal for Bell in front of 34,230.

SATURDAY 21ST SEPTEMBER 1991

Peter Beardsley, one of the most entertaining footballers in the late 1980s and early 1990s, scored a hat-trick as Everton won 3-0 at Goodison Park. Referee Alan Flood gave a debatable penalty for the third goal but by then the gates had opened and the blue side of Merseyside were pouring forward at will.

MONDAY 22ND SEPTEMBER 1947

Tommy Hutchison, who was voted the top Coventry player of the top-flight era, was born in Cardenden, Scotland. Signed from Blackpool in October 1972, Hutchison made 355 first-team appearances over nine seasons and scored 30 goals. His dazzling wing play and close ball control were a feature of his game and provided the ammunition for the likes of Ian Wallace and Mick Ferguson. He departed for Manchester City in the summer of 1981 and went on to score at both ends in the 1981 FA Cup Final against Tottenham Hotspur, playing alongside Dave Bennett, Bobby McDonald and Ray Ranson. During his time at Highfield Road, Hutchison won all 17 of his Scotland caps and played in the 1974 World Cup finals.

MONDAY 22ND SEPTEMBER 1958

Jimmy Rogers and Ray Straw shared seven goals as Coventry thrashed Aldershot Town 7-1 at Highfield Road. Rogers – who, similarly to Louis Carey signed from Bristol City and then re-signed three years later – scored four and shared the match ball with Straw. This was City's only season in Division Four as Billy Frith guided them to runners-up spot and an instant return to Division Three.

SATURDAY 22ND SEPTEMBER 2001

Just eight games into the season post Premier League, Portsmouth visited Highfield Road and their fans rampaged throughout the half-time interval. Prior to the game, there had been trouble in Coventry town centre and bus loads of Portsmouth supporters were herded into the ground where there were no police, only stewards. The second half was delayed while order was restored and the Sky Blues built on Jay Bothroyd's first-half opener with a second from Lee Carsley to win 2-0. Speaking to the *Coventry Evening Telegraph*, a police spokesperson said: "A number of so-called football supporters were interested in causing disorder. This sort of disgraceful behaviour will not be tolerated in the West Midlands and offenders can expect to be brought before the courts." Portsmouth chairman, Milan Mandaric, planned to root out the troublemakers: "I never want to see these people at Fratton Park again. I can't believe this has happened just when we're trying to calm down all the violence in the world. We're trying to heal wounds in the USA and this happens – it makes me sick." City caretaker manager Roland Nilsson agreed: "It is not something we want to see, especially after the terrible things that happened in New York recently."

SATURDAY 23RD SEPTEMBER 1995

The Sky Blues wore their new purple and gold away kit for the first time as they headed for Ewood Park. It would prove to be a 'no good luck omen' as they were comprehensively beaten 5-1 by Blackburn Rovers who had won the title the previous May. Peter Ndlovu missed a penalty then pulled a goal back as City trailed 2-1 at half-time. Unfortunately, the floodgates opened in the second half as further goals from Alan Shearer (two) and Ian Pearce capped a 5-1 victory. Local lad Iyseden Christie made his debut as substitute for Paul Cook and would go on to make two substitute appearances before forging a successful lower league career with a host of sides.

SATURDAY 24TH SEPTEMBER 2005

Hull City became the first side to win at the Ricoh Arena. John Welsh scored both goals as they won 2-0 in front of an impressive crowd of 21,149.

SATURDAY 25TH SEPTEMBER 1982

Signed in a swap deal with Tommy English, Jim Melrose joined the Sky Blues from Leicester City. The transfer was completed in time for him to make his debut against Everton at Highfield Road. The 4-2 scoreline was emphatic as City raced into a 4-1 lead after 67 minutes. Melrose fired a hat-trick on his debut with Steve Hunt notching the other goal. Future City assistant manager/caretaker manager Adrian Heath scored for Everton who also included Kevin Richardson in their starting eleven. When Keith Thompson replaced Steve Hunt towards the end, he lined up alongside brother Garry, the only time this would happen in sky blue colours.

WEDNESDAY 26TH SEPTEMBER 2007

On a memorable night at the 'Theatre of Dreams', the Sky Blues recorded a fabulous victory over the Premier League champions in the third round of the Carling Cup. With 74,055 packed into Old Trafford to see United's reserves, they lost 2-0 to Iain Dowie's inspired men. Prior to the game, Sir Alex Ferguson proudly spoke to the *Daily Mirror*: "Sit back and enjoy watching the emergence of some very special talent. Try to spot our stars of the future." Michael Mifsud scored both goals which shocked the United manager: "I was flabbergasted by our performance and I'm not even going to go into it. I certainly didn't expect that. We're all in a state of shock. These are all young players we've had great hope in and trumpeted in a loud way in recent years. So this is a big shock to us all." Iain Dowie said: "Having people like Wayne Rooney, Paul Scholes and Ryan Giggs missing was a bonus but Sir Alex put out a team that was good enough to win."

SATURDAY 27TH SEPTEMBER 1980

Four days after the 2-1 win at Brighton & Hove Albion in the third round of the League Cup, City crashed back down to earth with a rather large bump. Everton visited Highfield Road and were 3-0 ahead after half an hour. Two further second-half goals wrapped up the 5-0 win by the 70th minute. Future Sky Blue Bob Latchford (two), Joe McBride (two) and Peter Eastoe scored the goals which saw City slip to 15th position in Division One.

WEDNESDAY 27TH SEPTEMBER 2000

John Aloisi fired a hat-trick as City beat Preston North End 4-1 in the second round, second leg of the Worthington Cup. The victory gave the Sky Blues a 7-2 aggregate win and, during the relegation season, would be the only time Coventry hit four goals in any game. John Eustace completed the scoring and would score the winner in the next round at Southampton before Ipswich Town knocked City out in round four.

SATURDAY 28TH SEPTEMBER 1985

Popular former Sky Blue Steve Hunt returned to Highfield Road with West Bromwich Albion. In a tough season for the Baggies, they would win only four games all season and concede nearly 90 goals. City took them apart with goals from Micky Adams, Terry Gibson and Trevor Peake which sealed a 3-0 victory. It was too much for Hunt who was red carded for kicking out at Dave Bennett on his first return to the club that he served so well.

SATURDAY 28TH SEPTEMBER 1991

Peter Ndlovu scored one of his best City goals in the 1-0 win over Aston Villa at Highfield Road. A slalom style run ended with a left-foot shot which flew across Nigel Spink into the corner of the net. Big Cyrille Regis lined up for Villa, following his release from Coventry the previous May, along with Kevin Richardson and Steve Staunton in front of a low derby crowd of 17,831.

SATURDAY 29TH SEPTEMBER 1973

Les Cartwright joined the Sky Blues as an apprentice and made his debut as substitute in a 2-0 win over Leicester City at Filbert Street. Replacing Ernie Hunt, Cartwright scored on his debut, clinching the win with the second goal in the 70th minute. Between 1973 and 1977 he made 89 first-team appearances and scored seven goals before moving to Wrexham and then Cambridge United. While at City he was capped seven times by Wales and ended his career with a short loan spell at Nuneaton Borough.

WEDNESDAY 30TH SEPTEMBER 1908

Clarrie Bourton, Coventry City's leading goalscorer of all time, was born in Bristol. Quite simply, 182 goals in 241 first-team appearances is highly unlikely to ever be surpassed. Harry Storer signed him from Blackburn Rovers for £750 in 1931 and the rest, as they say, is history. His six seasons saw respective goal tallies of 50, 43, 25, 29, 26 (all in Division Three (South)) and nine (Division Two season) before he moved to Plymouth Argyle just after the start of season 1937/38. With the nearest modern-day goals tally held by Dion Dublin with 71 it could be a long time before any Sky Blues player comes remotely near Bourton's strike rate and total. A part of the Division Three (South) championship side in season 1935/36, Coventry scored an amazing 577 league goals during his City career, Bourton's tally a staggering 173. His career finished back at Bristol City and retirement came in 1944. From then he worked in the Ashton Gate side's Pools office until his death in April 1981, aged 72. Along with Cyrille Regis and Arthur Bacon, he holds the record for the highest number of goals scored in any one game – five – in the 6-1 win over Bournemouth in October 1931.

WEDNESDAY 30TH SEPTEMBER 1970

Trakia Plovdiv made the return journey for the second leg of the Fairs Cup tie. A crowd of 20,930 turned up at Highfield Road for the first-ever European night under the floodlights. Two first-half goals from Brian Joicey and Jeff Blockley sealed a 6-1 aggregate victory for the Sky Blues to progress into round two. The Bulgarians reside in the country's top division but have not faced English opponents since Coventry.

SATURDAY 30TH SEPTEMBER 1995

There would have been many supporters still taking their seats as City kicked off against Aston Villa at Highfield Road. Dwight Yorke turned the ball into the Coventry net after 13 seconds to stun the home crowd and take the sting out of the derby match. Further goals from Savo Milosevic completed a 3-0 win for Villa as they moved up to second in the table.

COVENTRY CITY
On This Day

OCTOBER

SATURDAY 1st OCTOBER 1988

A seven-goal thriller with Middlesbrough at Highfield Road saw David Speedie join Dion Dublin and Terry Bly in scoring a hat-trick but still ending up on the losing side. In a thrilling game, Speedie's hat-trick of headers was matched by the visitors' Bernie Slaven who rifled in a first-half hat-trick. Mark Burke made it 4-1 for Middlesbrough before Speedie gave the Sky Blues hope. It's not often you leave at the final whistle enthralled by what you have just seen having lost 4-3, but John Sillett's side entertained with width and pace and Speedie scored another hat-trick of headers in the 5-0 win over Sheffield Wednesday just after Christmas.

SATURDAY 2nd OCTOBER 1982

As rare as a back-pass punishment in modern-day football, Sky Blues goalkeeper Les Sealey fell foul of the 'four step' rule at Maine Road. As with all new laws introduced by the powers that be, referees were on the lookout for goalkeepers taking more than four steps while in possession of the ball. Sealey was punished by referee Keith Hackett, high profile as they came during the eighties, and a free kick was awarded to Manchester City inside the penalty area. With the score at 1-1, the late Tommy Caton smashed home the kick and turned the game on its head. Former City player David Cross made it 3-1 before Garry Thompson's consolation. Jim Melrose had opened the scoring in front of over 25,000 supporters.

WEDNESDAY 2nd OCTOBER 2002

The Sky Blues recorded their biggest cup victory with an 8-0 trouncing of Rushden & Diamonds at Highfield Road in the Worthington Cup second round. Gary McSheffrey's hat-trick usurped Lee Mills and Jay Bothroyd who both scored twice. Having joined as a trainee, Robert Betts scored the eighth from the penalty spot with his only senior goal for the club. The City side comprised Fabien Debec, Gary Caldwell, Barry Quinn, Youssef Safri, Mo Konjic, Calum Davenport, David Pipe, Gary McAllister, McSheffrey, Mills and Richie Partridge. Bothroyd replaced Mills while youngster Eddie Stanford replaced Richard Shaw in his only competitive outing for the club.

SUNDAY 3RD OCTOBER 1954

A product of Coventry's youth team, Mick Ferguson made his Sky Blues debut in a goalless draw at Elland Road against Leeds United in February 1975. Born in Newcastle-upon-Tyne on this day, Ferguson formed a fantastic partnership with Ian Wallace upon his arrival in 1976. His first spell in sky blue ended in 1981 when he signed for Everton having played 143 first-team games and scoring 55 goals. During season 1977/78 he scored 17 league goals in 30 league games, including three hat-tricks as the side shared 75 goals between them. In mid March 1984, Bobby Gould signed him on loan from Birmingham City and it is fair to say his goals kept City in Division One. Three vital strikes, including one in the 2-1 win over Norwich City, ensured safety and hero status.

SATURDAY 3RD OCTOBER 1970

Two goals from Ernie Hunt and one from Neil Martin gave the Sky Blues a 3-1 victory over Everton at Highfield Road. In the second half came a moment still revered today. Willie Carr's back heeled flick was volleyed into the visitors' net by Ernie Hunt and the legend of the 'donkey kick' was born.

SATURDAY 4TH OCTOBER 1980

Following the 5-0 thumping by Everton a week earlier, City raced into a three-goal lead against Brighton & Hove Albion after 64 minutes. Highfield Road was stunned into silence as Gordon Smith scored a hat-trick to level at 3-3 with three minutes remaining. Only 11,521 watched as the Sky Blues gifted the visitors a precious point in their fight for survival.

MONDAY 4TH OCTOBER 1993

Jim Holton made his Coventry debut in a 1-1 draw at West Bromwich Albion having signed from Sunderland in April 1977. Over the next four seasons he played 100 first-team games before injury brought premature retirement at the age of 30 in the summer of 1980. During the 1974 World Cup finals he wore the number five shirt in all three of Scotland's group games including the 0-0 draw with Brazil. He sadly died from a heart attack on this day aged just 42.

TUESDAY 5TH OCTOBER 1993

Freshly promoted from the Vauxhall Conference, Wycombe Wanderers trailed 3-0 after the first leg of this Coca Cola Cup tie at Highfield Road. Adams Park, a brand new stadium, welcomed the Sky Blues for the second leg on a cold October evening for more cup humiliation. Late extra-time goals from Steve Morgan and Phil Babb saved City's blushes after Wycombe raced into a 4-0 lead.

WEDNESDAY 6TH OCTOBER 1965

The first-ever game beamed live back to Highfield Road was set up by Jimmy Hill. City were at Ninian Park for a league clash with Cardiff City as closed circuit television relayed live pictures of the Sky Blues' 2-1 victory. Over 10,000 sat and watched the action on four large screens as George Curtis and Ronnie Rees scored the goals seen by the supporters in black and white.

FRIDAY 6TH OCTOBER 2006

The Ricoh Arena hosted its first-ever international match as England under-21s defeated their German counterparts 1-0. Everton's Leighton Baines scored the winner in the first leg of the European Under-21 Championship Qualifying Play-Off.

WEDNESDAY 7TH OCTOBER 1992

The McCain Stadium, Scarborough, hosted the Sky Blues just 12 months prior to the close shave against Wycombe Wanderers. This time the first leg saw goals from Brian Borrows and Peter Ndlovu tip the balance to sky blue as Bobby Gould's men headed to North Yorkshire. Goals from much travelled Tommy Mooney, Darren Foreman and Lee Hirst in the last 18 minutes, brought another calamity.

WEDNESDAY 8TH OCTOBER 1975

Field Mill, home of Mansfield Town, has always been a tricky place for top division sides visiting in the cup. Third Division Mansfield, with 10,000 supporters behind them, beat the Sky Blues 2-0 in the League Cup third-round tie. Clarke and Eccles scored the first-half goals as City caved in on a small pitch with the crowd right next to the touchline.

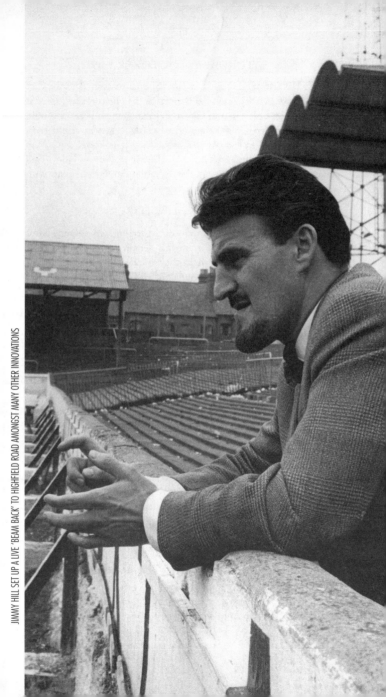

SATURDAY 9TH OCTOBER 1965

Jimmy Hill introduced the 'Sky Blue Special' to away days for City supporters. Coventry hired the train from the railways and staffed it with club stewards to ensure order was maintained. Wrecking train carriages had become a feature of match-day travel in recent years and Hill moved to combat this by making train travel supporter-friendly and gave the club's backing. The trip to Preston North End was the inaugural journey and the operation ran for four years with no problems whatsoever.

WEDNESDAY 9TH OCTOBER 1968

Sat in the relegation zone for most of the season, City suffered a 6-1 defeat at the hands of West Bromwich Albion in front of 29,926 at The Hawthorns. In a season where they would survive the drop by just one point and stay in the bottom half of Division One all season, this result was a crushing blow. Ernie Hunt gave Coventry hope at 3-1 but Albion wrapped up the win in style.

SATURDAY 9TH OCTOBER 1982

Tottenham Hotspur's Garry Brooke scored a six-minute hat-trick at White Hart Lane as the Sky Blues went 4-0 down after just 55 minutes. Midfielder Brooke added to Garth Crooks' opener with goals after 49, 50 and 55 minutes, the hat-trick clincher a retaken penalty after Les Sealey had saved the initial effort. Dave Sexton's men were indebted to Sealey as the Londoners ran riot.

WEDNESDAY 9TH OCTOBER 1985

Following a 2-1 win at Chester City in the Milk Cup first round first leg, it all came together for Cyrille Regis in the second leg. Five goals from Big Cyrille, four before half-time, were added to by Terry Gibson and Brian Kilcline as Chester were thrashed 7-2. Regis equalled the feat by Clarrie Bourton and Arthur Bacon in the early 1930s and took City to a 9-3 aggregate win. The shame for Cyrille was only 5,510 were present to watch his feat as Coventry moved to a third-round tie with West Bromwich Albion where they would lose 4-3 after a replay.

SATURDAY 10TH OCTOBER 1964

The Sky Blues' new electronic scoreboard celebrated its first display of a City victory with the 3-2 win over Swindon Town. At the fourth time of asking since its debut in the 2-0 defeat to Derby County three weeks previously, a City home win was finally displayed for all to see. Ken Hale, Ernie Machin and George Hudson scored the goals in front of 25,216 fans.

SATURDAY 11TH OCTOBER 1975

Arsenal finished the previous season in 16th position, two places below Coventry. They would struggle again in 1975/76 but saved one of their best performances for the visit of Gordon Milne's men. Alex Cropley and Brian Kidd both notched doubles with Alan Ball completing the 5-0 thumping at Highbury. Bryan King was between the City posts that day as the Gunners ran riot.

SATURDAY 11TH OCTOBER 1980

As one of City's best-ever right-backs Graham Oakey announced his premature retirement at the age of just 26, the Sky Blues went to Filbert Street and outplayed local rivals Leicester City. Paul Dyson, Ray Gooding and a late Tommy English clincher sandwiched Gary Lineker's strike for the Foxes as the City supporters travelled back along the M69 having savoured a 3-1 win.

WEDNESDAY 12TH OCTOBER 1983

England kept their faint hopes of Euro 84 qualification alive by winning 3-0 in Budapest against Hungary in the famous Nep Stadium. In their penultimate qualifying game, top spot was held by Denmark who would lose to France in the semi-final of the tournament the following June. Glenn Hoddle, Sammy Lee and Paul Mariner scored before half-time to ensure a second-half stroll for Bobby Robson's men. The England side contained three men who would play a part in the future of Coventry as full-backs Phil Neal and Mick Mills lined up alongside Terry Butcher in defence. Mills assisted Butcher during his reign as Sky Blues' manager and departed shortly before the England legend left the club, replaced by Don Howe who assisted Bobby Robson throughout his England tenure.

SATURDAY 13TH OCTOBER 1956

Making his Coventry debut in the number seven shirt, Steve Mokone became the first-ever black player to pull on a City shirt in the 2-1 home defeat to Millwall. Born in South Africa on March 23rd 1938, winger Mokone picked up the nickname 'Kalamazoo' while at City. Mokone made four first-team appearances for the Bantams and scored a solitary goal during this time. He moved to Holland in 1958 before returning to play for Cardiff City and the little matter of Barcelona, Marseille and Torino before retiring in 1964.

SUNDAY 13TH OCTOBER 1996

City and Southampton shared a point with a 1-1 draw at Highfield Road. Dion Dublin's injury-time goal cancelled out another piece of genius from Matt Le Tissier. The match was noticeable for Ron Atkinson's use of three substitutes for the first time since the introduction in the summer. Paul Williams, Peter Ndlovu and Dublin replaced Brian Borrows, David Burrows and Eoin Jess as the Sky Blues looked to get back into the game.

SATURDAY 14TH OCTOBER 1950

Coventry went top of Division Two with a 6-1 thumping of Blackburn Rovers at Highfield Road. Bryn Allen and Norman Lockhart both scored twice with Ted Roberts and Ken Chisholm completing the scoring. A crowd of 34,915 watched the goal feast as City eventually wound up seventh in the table.

SATURDAY 15TH OCTOBER 1977

Referee Clive Thomas awarded four penalty kicks in the Sky Blues' 2-1 win at Filbert Street. Two David Webb handballs were punished with unerring accuracy by Mick Coop. Jim Blyth saved Dennis Rofe's spot kick before he was finally beaten from 12 yards by Jon Sammels.

TUESDAY 15TH OCTOBER 1985

The Southern Section of the Full Members' Cup saw Millwall visit Highfield Road in the first round of the newly formed competition. Enthusiasm was not high amongst the supporters which explained why the smallest attendance since the war, 1,086, watched a 1-1 draw. Terry Gibson scored the Sky Blues' goal.

WEDNESDAY 16TH OCTOBER 1968

The Sky Blues forced a replay in the fourth round of the League Cup at home to Swindon Town. Only four minutes remained as the visitors led 2-0 through goals from Don Rogers and Roger Smart. John Tudor gave City hope before Tony Hateley took the tie to a replay with an 88th-minute header. The Wiltshire side won the replay 3-1 at the County Ground and would go on to play Arsenal in the final where they triumphed 3-1 after extra time. Former City player and manager, Bobby Gould, equalised for Arsenal to take the tie to a further 30 minutes.

SATURDAY 16TH OCTOBER 1999

Coventry romped to a 4-1 win at Highfield Road against Newcastle United. Inspired by a resurgent Gary McAllister, goals from Paul Williams, Carlton Palmer, Robbie Keane and Moustapha Hadji were too much for a Newcastle side reduced to ten men after Warren Barton's sending off in the first half. Manager Gordon Strachan sang his captain's praises as he spoke to the *Daily Mirror*: "Gary received a great reception from the fans when I substituted him at the end because he has been in brilliant form this season. This is the first time in seven years he has not had to carry the burden of being Scotland's captain. He is now actually getting a rest which I think is the right thing for him to do. I was exactly the same." The visitors' manager, Bobby Robson, was furious with Barton: "The game was lost the moment he was sent off. He's very upset with himself and it was out of character."

SATURDAY 17TH OCTOBER 1931

On his way to smashing a club-record 50 goals in a season, Clarrie Bourton scored the first of seven hat-tricks in a 6-1 win against Bournemouth at Highfield Road. Bill Shepherd completed the scoring as Bourton helped himself to five goals en route to setting a record that exists to this day, and is highly unlikely to be bettered. What is amazing to see is that over 100 league goals were scored by Harry Storer's side yet they finished only 12th. Bourton scored in ten successive matches during the autumn. Defences found him unplayable.

SATURDAY 18TH OCTOBER 1919

After nine successive defeats at the start of City's Football League tenure, they secured their first-ever point with a 0-0 draw at Craven Cottage against Fulham. Supporters would have to wait until Christmas Day for the first victory, a 3-2 win at home against Stoke City. Following five draws and 14 defeats, the points were long overdue. Boxing Day saw Coventry play Stoke City at the Victoria Ground and the Potters won 6-1 in the days when fixture scheduling was not dictated by the television companies or compiled by the Football Association's computer.

SATURDAY 18TH OCTOBER 1958

Two goals from Ray Straw saw City take the points with a win over Northampton Town at Highfield Road. Home form is essential to any successful campaign and Coventry lost only once on home turf as they ensured only one year would be spent in Division Four following the Football League's restructuring. Straw made 158 first-team appearances and scored 87 goals during his four seasons at Highfield Road. Each season he was top scorer and contributed 27 during the promotion year. As City began life in Division Three, Straw became the first player to play in all six divisions of the league.

WEDNESDAY 18TH OCTOBER 1961

Another product of the fine youth policy under Gordon Milne, Tommy English was born in Cirencester on this day. English made his debut in the 3-2 defeat at Stoke City on the opening day of season 1979/80, aged 17. A centre forward, English found himself in direct competition with Ian Wallace and Mick Ferguson, and then Garry Thompson and Mark Hateley, for a first-team striking berth. He scored on his home debut in the next match against Bristol City and went on to make 76 first-team appearances with 22 goals to his name. In October 1982 he moved to Leicester City to rejoin Milne in the deal which saw Jim Melrose join the Sky Blues. One memory of English is seeing him take to the pitch sporting dyed blonde hair which was rarely seen on a football pitch in 1981. His career took him to Rochdale, Plymouth Argyle and Colchester United before moving into non-league.

SATURDAY 19TH OCTOBER 1963

During a season which would end with the raising of the Division Three championship trophy, City suffered a rare defeat at Layer Road as Colchester United won 2-1. Only eight matches were lost all season as Jimmy Hill's men swept all before them. Willie Humphries scored the Sky Blues' goal in front of just 7,189.

SATURDAY 19TH OCTOBER 1974

The Sky Blues fought back from 2-1, 3-2 and 4-3 to share eight goals in a thriller with Middlesbrough at Ayresome Park. Gordon Milne's men took on newly promoted Boro under Jack Charlton and took a point with goals from Colin Stein, David Cross and a double from Jimmy Holmes.

SATURDAY 20TH OCTOBER 1923

Manager Albert Evans' City side left the field at Bloomfield Road, Blackpool, on the end of a 5-0 defeat in Division Two. Prior to the fixtures computer, City did not have to wait long to wreak revenge on the Tangerines as seven days later they won 3-1 at Highfield Road.

TUESDAY 20TH OCTOBER 1970

Franz Beckenbauer, Sepp Maier, Gerd Muller and company welcomed Coventry to Munich as City's reward for beating Trakia Plovdiv was the soon-to-be-great West German side, Bayern Munich. The European Fairs Cup second round, first leg, saw the tie effectively ended as a contest as the Sky Blues lost 6-1. Goals from Muller (two), Schneider (two), Roth and Schwarzenbeck, in front of 12,548 hardy souls, does not reflect Ernie Hunt's equaliser on 12 minutes yet by half time a 4-1 lead had been built and the tie taken out of City's grasp.

MONDAY 20TH OCTOBER 1997

The Sky cameras were at Oakwell as newly promoted Barnsley won 2-0 on a wet and windy Yorkshire evening against Gordon Strachan's men. Ashley Ward and Neil Redfearn scored the goals as a Coventry attack without Dublin and Huckerby struggled with their hosts' direct approach and Barnsley took the three points. The season would prove to be their one and only top-flight campaign.

SATURDAY 21ST OCTOBER 1933

Billy Lake scored the equalising goal as City drew 1-1 at the Goldstone Ground against Brighton & Hove Albion. Lake joined Coventry from Walsall in November 1928 and played for 11 seasons, between the two world wars. He made a total of 245 first-team appearances and his 123 goals rank him second only to Clarrie Bourton in the all-time leading scorers.

SATURDAY 21ST OCTOBER 1978

Mick Ferguson scored the Sky Blues' goal at West Bromwich Albion in the 69th minute. In the 68 minutes prior, Albion scored four and added three more after Ferguson's consolation to rout City 7-1. Future Sky Blue Cyrille Regis scored twice, as did the late Laurie Cunningham. Len Cantello, Tony Brown and Derek Statham completed the scoring as Ron Atkinson's all-star cast displayed the form that took them to a final placing of third.

SATURDAY 22ND OCTOBER 1932

Jock Lauderdale added to two goals from Clarrie Bourton as Coventry drew 3-3 at Loftus Road against Queens Park Rangers. Lauderdale joined the club under Harry Storer's management in the summer of 1931 and dovetailed with Bourton to great effect as the side scored goals for fun and entertained the fans. His six seasons at Highfield Road saw him find the back of the net 63 times in 182 matches leaving him tenth in the all-time scorers list. Following promotion to Division Two he moved to Northampton Town.

TUESDAY 22ND OCTOBER 1963

The Sky Blues thrashed Shrewsbury Town 8-1 at Highfield Road as George Hudson (two) added to Ronnie Rees' hat-trick. Hubert Barr (two), and an own goal, continued the push for promotion under Jimmy Hill. Hill signed Hudson from Peterborough United in the spring of 1963 to replace Terry Bly and set a new club-record transfer fee of £21,000. Seventh in City's all-time scorers list, Hudson scored 75 goals for Coventry in just 129 matches yet missed out on playing for the Sky Blues in Division One when he was sold to Northampton Town in the spring of 1966.

SATURDAY 23RD OCTOBER 1993

Bobby Gould's final match in charge during his second spell as Coventry manager saw Les Ferdinand and company take the Sky Blues apart as they roared to a 5-1 victory at Loftus Road. Ferdinand and a double from Bradley Allen left the Sky Blues trailing 3-0 at half-time with a fourth added by future Sky Blue Andy Impey. Peter Ndlovu gave the travelling support something to cheer with a late consolation before Simon Barker made it 5-1.

SATURDAY 24TH OCTOBER 1942

George Mason scored one of the Coventry goals as they drew 2-2 at Highfield Road against Birmingham City. Born on September 5th 1913, Mason made his City debut in a 3-1 defeat to Bristol Rovers in March 1932 and played until his release in 1952 – twenty years – with World War II to take into account. In total, he appeared 350 times and scored eight goals. In 1936 he lifted the Division Three championship trophy and played under Harry Storer (twice), Dick Bayliss and Billy Frith.

SATURDAY 24TH OCTOBER 1981

Swansea City made the most of their first-ever top-flight season and visited Highfield Road leading the pack. The game was over shortly after half-time as goals from Mark Hateley (two) and Rudi Kaiser gave the Swans no way back. Kaiser's goal was his third in a City shirt, having joined in the summer, and his wing play entertained out on the right side of midfield. He made 19 first-team appearances and scored three goals during his brief stay.

SATURDAY 24TH OCTOBER 1987

Highfield Road witnessed the magic of Paul Gascoigne as the footballing genius inspired Newcastle United to a 3-1 victory. Cyrille Regis replied to Paul Goddard's opening goal before Gazza and Darren Jackson sealed the three points.

SATURDAY 25TH OCTOBER 1969

Champions elect, Everton, displayed smash and grab tendencies as Joe Royle's 87th-minute goal took the points at Highfield Road. In the return at Goodison Park, City held the Toffees to a goalless draw.

SATURDAY 25TH OCTOBER 1975

Soon to be Sky Blue, Terry Yorath, opened the scoring for Leeds United in their 2-0 win at Elland Road. Allan Clarke sealed the victory in front of 25,956 Yorkshiremen about to realise the glory days would soon be over.

SATURDAY 25TH OCTOBER 1986

Lee Chapman's double was cancelled out by Cyrille Regis and Steve Ogrizovic as Hillsborough witnessed the City custodian drop-kick the ball over his opposite number Martin Hodge. The 2-2 draw was memorable for Oggy's feat in front of 20,035. Supporters not at the game watched in disbelief as 'Ogrizovic 63' flashed up before their eyes on teletext to seal a point and take City up to sixth in Division One.

SATURDAY 26TH OCTOBER 1918

The season prior to joining the Football League, Coventry thrashed Huddersfield Town 7-1 at Highfield Road. Just seven days previously, the Yorkshire side had triumphed 4-1 at Leeds Road. Buckley, Howell, Lowes and Middlemiss complemented a hat-trick from Chris Sambrooke who went on to score 23 goals by the end of the season.

SATURDAY 26TH OCTOBER 1985

Terry Gibson marked his 100th game in Coventry colours with the only goal at St. Andrew's as Ron Saunders' men continued their plummet towards relegation. Birmingham's side included David Seaman, City chairman Ray Ranson and former Sky Blues Brian Roberts and Jim Hagan with Nicky Platnauer on the substitutes' bench. Gibson would be sold to Manchester United in February in a swap with Alan Brazil.

SATURDAY 26TH OCTOBER 1996

Ron Atkinson's final game as Coventry manager saw him face one of his former sides as Sheffield Wednesday shared a point in a 0-0 draw. City remained in 19th position, where they had started the season, and Atkinson moved 'upstairs' to make way for his assistant manager, Gordon Strachan, to assume command. Atkinson's final side comprised Steve Ogrizovic, Paul Williams, John Salako, Kevin Richardson, Liam Daish, Richard Shaw, Paul Telfer, Gary McAllister, Dion Dublin, Noel Whelan and Peter Ndlovu.

TUESDAY 27TH OCTOBER 1981

Just eight months after falling to West Ham United in the League Cup semi-finals, the Sky Blues bowed out at the first hurdle to an Everton attack led by former City great Mick Ferguson. City's former number nine only departed in the summer and scored the opening goal in the first leg at Goodison Park before Mark Hateley's late leveller. In the second leg back at his old stomping ground, Ferguson netted with just five minutes remaining in front of a stunned home support.

SATURDAY 27TH OCTOBER 2001

In the middle of a ten-game unbeaten run, Roland Nilsson's men topped Division One, just six months after relegation from the Premier League. Youssef Safri and Lee Hughes with a penalty kick gave City the three points in front of 17,381 against a Sheffield Wednesday side also smarting from relegation in recent years. Norwegian Runar Normann and Honduran Jairo Martinez came off the substitutes' bench to face a Wednesday side in the caretaker charge of former City star Terry Yorath.

SATURDAY 28TH OCTOBER 1939

The outbreak of World War II led to season 1939/40 being halted after just three games. On September 3rd, war was declared and competitive football matches stopped. Seven weeks later regional friendly matches were permitted to be played and Coventry participated in the Regional League Midland Division. West Bromwich Albion visited Highfield Road on this day and suffered a 6-3 defeat as Billy Frith bagged a hat-trick, complemented by a double from Tommy Green and one from George Lowrie. Lowrie had been signed from Preston North End only three months before the war began and scored on his debut in the last game prior to the call. When he moved to Newcastle United in 1948, he had scored 59 goals in only 85 first-team appearances.

SATURDAY 28TH OCTOBER 2006

Introduced as a substitute for Leon McKenzie, Wayne Andrews scored with his first touch of the ball as the Sky Blues won 1-0 at Barnsley. By the time the Oakwell public address had announced the change, Andrews was wheeling away in celebration.

SATURDAY 29TH OCTOBER 1966

Bobby Gould scored the only goal as the Sky Blues beat Charlton Athletic 1-0 in front of just under 20,000 fans at Highfield Road. Coventry's home record was the key to clinching promotion into Division One with only one home defeat all season, Crystal Palace, as fortress Highfield Road became a difficult venue for opposing sides.

SATURDAY 29TH OCTOBER 1977

Mick Ferguson scored one of his three hat-tricks in 1977/78 as the Sky Blues turned in an excellent performance to triumph 3-1 at Molineux. Future Sky Blue Kenny Hibbitt opened the scoring before Ferguson's second-half trio took the two points back to Coventry. The win maintained the Sky Blues' sixth-place in a season where they would hold their top half position throughout. Gordon Milne's side comprised Jim Blyth, Graham Oakey, Bobby McDonald, Terry Yorath, John Beck, Mick Coop, Don Nardiello, Ian Wallace, Ferguson, Barry Powell and Tommy Hutchison.

SATURDAY 29TH OCTOBER 1988

The climax to season 1988/89 saw Arsenal's Michael Thomas clinch the title in the very last minute of the campaign up at Anfield. It was goalscoring form he had displayed throughout the season and the Sky Blues bore the brunt of his midfield skills as he strode forward to smash a 25-yard strike into the top corner. Tony Adams added a late second as the Gunners built up a head of steam for their title push. Running the show yet again for Arsenal was David Rocastle, who always played well against the Sky Blues. In March 2001, he died at the age of 33 from non-Hodgkin's lymphoma, an aggressive form of cancer.

SATURDAY 30TH OCTOBER 1965

Goals from George Hudson, Dudley Roberts and a Ron Farmer penalty gave Coventry a 3-2 victory over Portsmouth as Jimmy Hill's revolution continued. City would end the season in third place and just missed out on promotion to Division One. This would have to wait 12 months and the crowd of just over 25,000 had just witnessed a third straight City win.

TUESDAY 30TH OCTOBER 2007

Sky sent their cameras to the Ricoh Arena for the fourth-round Carling Cup clash with Premier League West Ham United. Just how cruel a game football is was displayed here as a Marcus Hall own goal levelled the score at 1-1 as extra time loomed. A debatable challenge by Carlton Cole on Ben Turner saw the ball break kindly for the young striker and he calmly side-footed into the net in the 92nd minute. There was barely time for the game to restart as City bowed out.

SATURDAY 31ST OCTOBER 1931

Born on the City side of Bristol, Clarrie Bourton would doubtless have enjoyed scoring the City goal in the 1-1 draw with Bristol Rovers at Highfield Road. He would score in the return fixture at Eastville but the blue side of Bristol walked away with a 3-1 victory. Over the years Bourton had an excellent record against both Bristol sides including four in the club's 9-0 record win against City.

SATURDAY 31ST OCTOBER 1953

Floodlights made their debut at Highfield Road as Coventry welcomed Queen of the South for a friendly match in front of 16,923 curious spectators.

SATURDAY 31ST OCTOBER 1992

Four years before he joined the Sky Blues, Gary McAllister got his name amongst the City scorers when he headed Lee Hurst's corner into his own net at Elland Road. Peter Ndlovu scored City's other goal before Chris Fairclough and Lee Chapman levelled at 2-2. Irish youngster Tony Sheridan made his Coventry debut in the number seven shirt before being replaced by Phil Babb. Sheridan would make just five full appearances with four as substitute before being released in the summer of 1995.

SUNDAY 31ST OCTOBER 1993

Phil Neal's first match as Coventry manager welcomed both Sheffield United and the Sky cameras to Highfield Road. With the departed Bobby Gould working as a guest pundit for Sky the game ended in a 0-0 draw.

COVENTRY CITY
On This Day

NOVEMBER

WEDNESDAY 1st NOVEMBER 2000

With one minute of extra time remaining John Eustace fired in the winner to take City through to the fourth round of the Worthington Cup. An 11,809 crowd were at The Dell as the Sky Blues ended Southampton's hopes of silverware for another season.

TUESDAY 1st NOVEMBER 2005

With the Sky Blues perilously close to the drop zone, it came as something of a relief when Plymouth Argyle's home clash with Leicester City was abandoned as rain stopped play. With Argyle leading 1-0, Coventry were in the bottom three but the elements conspired to assist City. Fast forward to May as Dennis Wise-inspired Coventry ended the season in eighth position, 21 points off the relegation zone.

SATURDAY 2nd NOVEMBER 1901

Coventry suffered their biggest FA Cup defeat as they took on Worcester-based Berwick Rangers in the second qualifying round. Berwick even gifted City an own goal as they scored 11 of their own. It is highly unlikely this defeat will ever be bettered, if that is the right word; 11-2 would take some eclipsing.

SATURDAY 3rd NOVEMBER 1951

Lol Harvey made his Coventry debut in a 1-0 defeat at Griffin Park to Brentford. Born on the 25th July 1934, Harvey played for City over nine seasons and was part of the side which gained promotion from Division Four. He made 149 first-team appearances and scored twice before retiring through injury at the age of just 27.

TUESDAY 3rd NOVEMBER 1970

Coventry City 2 Bayern Munich 1, as the four-time future winners of the European Cup visited the West Midlands. Next morning, the newspapers reported a 7-3 aggregate win for the West German side but the Sky Blues had their moment of glory in the Fairs Cup second-round second leg. Neil Martin and John O'Rourke made the headlines as Uli Hoeness netted for Bayern. The top stars turned out for Bayern and graced Highfield Road in front of 26,033 fans.

TUESDAY 4TH NOVEMBER 1980

Following a 1-1 draw at Highfield Road in the League Cup fourth round, the Sky Blues headed for the Abbey Stadium to take on Cambridge United in the replay. City followers may have been forgiven for thinking the best chance of progression had gone but Gordon Milne's young side had other ideas. Steve Hunt fired the winner shortly before half-time to take City into a fifth-round tie at Watford. Les Sealey saved Cambridge midfielder Steve Spriggs' penalty on the hour as United poured forward to retrieve the deficit as they had done in the first tie. A crowd of 10,171 packed into the small ground and left disappointed as City celebrated.

SATURDAY 4TH NOVEMBER 1989

Leaders Liverpool would go on to win the title by nine points from Arsenal but suffered their only home defeat against the mighty Sky Blues. Cyrille Regis' 47th-minute goal took the three points to stun the Kop and move Coventry up to ninth in Division One. Former Liverpool midfielder Kevin Macdonald wore the number four shirt for the Sky Blues and spoke to the *Daily Mirror* as he summed up the win: "It was a great experience to come back here and win. We rode our luck and went out to try to shut them down and it worked. People talk about a crisis but Liverpool are still the best. It was great to win but it wouldn't surprise me if Liverpool went the rest of the season without losing another game. I reckon they will be champions at the end of the season." A fuming Kenny Dalglish said: "The players' attitude wasn't right. The coaches can't do anything about passing, control and movement. Once the players are out there they have got to do that for themselves and they didn't." Steve Ogrizovic kept a rare clean sheet at Anfield and joked: "It was like the Alamo in that last 20 minutes."

MONDAY 4TH NOVEMBER 1996

The Sky cameras captured Gordon Strachan's first unofficial game in charge of the Sky Blues. City travelled to Goodison Park and came away with a creditable 1-1 draw. A Graham Poll awarded penalty was despatched by Graham Stuart before Gary McAllister struck from range to level.

WEDNESDAY 5TH NOVEMBER 2003

The plan to play on Bonfire Night backfired spectacularly as City supporters endured a woeful performance as Bradford City visited. Highfield Road was a cacophony of air bombs and rockets as the smoke-surrounded stadium endured a goalless draw in front of 11,871 fans.

MONDAY 6TH NOVEMBER 2006

The Sky cameras just about picked out Andy Griffin's Goal of the Season contender at a fog-bound Britannia Stadium. Stoke held on for the three points, even when reduced to ten men, after Ricardo Fuller's elbow on Michael Doyle.

TUESDAY 7TH NOVEMBER 1961

Mark Hateley came through the youth ranks at Coventry and made his debut in the final game of season 1978/79, a 3-0 win over Wolverhampton Wanderers at Highfield Road. Born in Wallasey, Merseyside on this day, Hateley made 111 first-team appearances for the club and scored 34 goals, before he departed along with so many others in the summer of 1983. Portsmouth signed him for £190,000 to take him into Division Two before his goal in Rio for England catapulted him into Serie 'A' and three seasons with AC Milan.

THURSDAY 8TH NOVEMBER 1956

Highfield Road hosted a Division Three (South) versus Division Three (North) match in the days when Division Three was split into two leagues. Coventry's Reg Matthews wore the number one shirt for the South, who were managed by City's manager Harry Warren, and triumphed 2-1. These representative games were a feature between 1954 and 1958 until the league was restructured in the summer of 1958.

SATURDAY 8TH NOVEMBER 1958

City's sole season in Division Four saw only ten games lost as the title trophy was lifted. One of these defeats was a 2-0 reverse to Bradford City at Valley Parade in front of 8,619 fans. In future years the Yorkshire side would leave the Premier League the same season as the Sky Blues and then plummet swiftly to League Two, the very old Division Four.

SATURDAY 8TH NOVEMBER 1997

Having collected a cross, Newcastle United goalkeeper Shay Given rolled the ball out in preparation to launch it downfield. He hadn't banked on the craftiness of City's Dion Dublin, lurking on his blind side. As Given prepared to kick, Dublin appeared from behind him to nick the ball and side-foot into the net for a perfectly legal goal. In the years since there have been a number of similar examples all inspired by Dublin's moment of genius. Dublin scored his second later in the game but goals from John Barnes and Robert Lee ensured the spoils were shared at Highfield Road. Of the respective line-ups on show that day, only Given and Marcus Hall are still playing professional football; Given at cash laden Manchester City, Hall recently released by the Sky Blues.

SATURDAY 9TH NOVEMBER 1935

Coventry's Division Three (South) title-winning side won 24 out of their 42 league games. Their biggest win came at Highfield Road as Crystal Palace were thumped 8-1. Inevitably, Clarrie Bourton notched a hat-trick and there were doubles for Leslie Jones and George McNestry. Jock Lauderdale completed the rout as just under 21,000 watched the entertainers at work. Jones would score 73 goals in 145 first-team appearances to leave him eighth in Coventry's all-time goalscorers list. He spent five seasons at Highfield Road and was transferred to Arsenal in 1937 by manager Harry Storer. While at Arsenal he won a title medal and added to the five Welsh international caps he collected at Coventry, ending his career with eleven.

SATURDAY 10TH NOVEMBER 1990

John Sillett's final match in charge of the Sky Blues took him to Roker Park as City fought out a 0-0 draw with Sunderland. Only Steve Ogrizovic, Brian Borrows, Dean Emerson, Trevor Peake, Michael Gynn and Cyrille Regis remained from his Wembley era squad just three-and-a-half years on from Coventry's greatest day for which he will be forever remembered.

SATURDAY 11TH NOVEMBER 1967

Fulham would finish the season bottom of Division One and claimed a rare win as they won 3-0 at Highfield Road. Their side included Johnny Haynes, George Cohen and Allan 'Sniffer' Clarke. It was Clarke who scored twice to add to Joe Gilroy's early strike. The Sky Blues would finish their debut season just one place and one point above the Division One relegation zone as Manchester City claimed the title.

SATURDAY 11TH NOVEMBER 1978

Referee David Hutchinson solved visibility issues with the introduction of an orange ball as City took on Middlesbrough at Highfield Road. Ian Wallace's early goal was cancelled out by the visitors' Micky Burns before Garry Thompson sent the crowd home happy with an 88th-minute winner.

SUNDAY 12TH NOVEMBER 1961

Danny Thomas, who made his debut against West Bromwich Albion in a 2-1 League Cup defeat at The Hawthorns, was born in Worksop, Nottinghamshire. Right-back Thomas collected two England caps while at City on a summer tour to Australia in June 1983. His stock rose and two months later Tottenham Hotspur signed him for £300,000. During his time at Coventry he made 130 first-team appearances and scored six goals. In March 1987, he missed out on a Wembley reunion with his old teammates after a shocking tackle in a match against Queens Park Rangers ended his career aged just 26. He now runs his own physiotherapy practice in Coventry.

SATURDAY 12TH NOVEMBER 1977

Third in the all-time appearance list, Mick Coop marked his 300th appearance at Highbury by scoring an own goal past Jim Blyth. The 31,653 crowd watched Malcolm Macdonald sent off shortly after Alan Green had given the Sky Blues a third-minute lead.

SATURDAY 12TH NOVEMBER 1988

Graham Rodger scored the winner as the Sky Blues beat Luton Town 1-0 at Highfield Road. Former Sky Blues Les Sealey and Ashley Grimes lined up for Luton who would sign Rodger in the summer of 1989.

WEDNESDAY 13TH NOVEMBER 1996

Gillingham's right-back Neil Smith rocked Highfield Road with the only goal as the Kent side reached the fourth round of the Coca Cola Cup. The Division Three side scored in the 71st minute as 12,639 watched in disbelief. The game was Gordon Strachan's first official match as Coventry manager and even a late cameo from the man himself failed to inspire the side.

THURSDAY 14TH NOVEMBER 1940

The city of Coventry was hit by 515 German bombers on this evening as more than 4,000 homes were destroyed along with the majority of the city's factories. There was barely a building left undamaged in the city centre and over 600 people died with many others injured. High explosive and incendiary bombs were dropped on the city by the bombers as the cathedral was damaged beyond repair. The raid would be the worst to hit Coventry during the war.

WEDNESDAY 15TH NOVEMBER 2006

Following the 2-1 defeat to Derby County at the Ricoh Arena, manager Micky Adams outlined to the *Coventry Evening Telegraph* where he thought it had gone wrong: "The marking could possibly have been tighter for the first goal but Jon Stead was playing on the left-hand side and we allowed him to wheel in a header from Steve Howard, and to be fair to the boy, he struck it well into the top corner. But maybe the defending could have been better. With the results that have gone our way, the confidence is not there at the moment but I do feel that in key moments in games we are not taking our chances. But, I have been in this situation before, particularly at this football club, and we have got to ride it out and keep going." Stern John levelled Jon Stead's strike before Steve Howard powered home a header from a corner to take the points back to the East Midlands. Derby went on to be promoted via the play-offs to the Premier League but their moment in the spotlight was short lived. They were relegated with the lowest points tally having managed to win only one game all season, a home victory against Newcastle United.

TUESDAY 16TH NOVEMBER 1971

Gordon Strachan broke the club transfer record when he signed Moustapha Hadji from Deportivo La Coruna for £4 million. Born in Ifrane, Morocco, Hadji made his debut in a 1-0 defeat to Southampton at Highfield Road on the opening day of season 1999/00 along with fellow Moroccan Youssef Chippo. Two seasons later, following relegation, he moved to Aston Villa having made 70 first-team appearances, and scored 13 goals. He represented Morocco in the 1994 and 1998 World Cup finals but his final act in sky blue was to score both goals at Villa Park before his future employers hit back to end City's top-flight existence.

SATURDAY 16TH NOVEMBER 1985

Following the controversial introduction of their artificial pitch at Kenilworth Road, Luton Town's home record improved immeasurably. In its inaugural season, only three games were lost; the Sky Blues took the honour of being the first visitors to triumph on the uneven-bounced sand trap. Players had to wear trainers on the surface and incurred abrasions aplenty as the Hatters took advantage of training on it every day. David Bowman's first-half strike took the three points back to the West Midlands, a haul that would prove extremely valuable as City finished just two points off relegation in 17th place. Former City custodian Les Sealey dropped a clanger for Bowman's goal while brief future City match-winner, Mick Harford, led the Hatters' front line.

SUNDAY 17TH NOVEMBER 1963

Midfield playmaker Isaias Marques Soares became the first Brazilian to play in the Premier League when he signed from Benfica in the summer of 1995. His profile soared after a stunning display for Benfica at Highbury in the 1991 European Cup as he scored twice to send Arsenal out of the competition. Born in Rio de Janeiro, Ron Atkinson signed him for £500,000 and his debut came against Manchester City at Highfield Road in August 1995. Fitness was a problem and contributed to him making just 14 appearances in his 18 months at the club. His two goals came away from Highfield Road; one at Stamford Bridge, the other at the Riverside.

SATURDAY 17TH NOVEMBER 1979

A male streaker interrupted play and the concentration of the Wolverhampton Wanderers' defence as City strode to a 3-0 victory. The home side finished the season in sixth position and added the League Cup to the trophy cabinet with Andy Gray's goal at Wembley defeating Nottingham Forest. Ian Wallace, and two from Mick Ferguson, gave City the two points in a season where they would win just four times on their travels.

SATURDAY 17TH NOVEMBER 1990

Terry Butcher's first game as player-manager of Coventry welcomed champions Liverpool to Highfield Road. Having taken over from John Sillett on the Wednesday, 32-year-old Butcher stepped up from being a first-team regular at Glasgow Rangers to line up alongside Peter Billing and Trevor Peake in a back five. With 22,496 packed into the stadium, a tight game was decided when Butcher and Steve Ogrizovic collided to leave Peter Beardsley an easy winner. In 15th position when he took control, Coventry ended the season one place lower, ten points off the drop. As a Coventry player, Terry Butcher appeared just seven times in his first season and retired the following November following a red card in a Zenith Data Systems Cup tie against Aston Villa.

SATURDAY 18TH NOVEMBER 1950

Third in the list of all-time Coventry goalscorers, Ted Roberts scored City's second goal in the 5-4 defeat to Southampton at The Dell in a Division Two fixture. Bryn Allen, Ken Chisholm and Norman Lockhart completed the scoring for City in front of 22,438. Between March 1937 and 1952, Roberts scored 87 goals in 223 first-team appearances after signing from Derby County. His debut came at Turf Moor, shortly after joining the club, but then World War II interrupted his career; he was 22 when war started and 29 when it finished in 1946.

SATURDAY 19TH NOVEMBER 1927

Millwall inflicted Coventry's second-biggest league defeat of all time with a 9-1 victory at Cold Blow Lane. Scotsman Peter Ramage scored the City goal in a season where they lost 21 out of 42 league games to finish 20th in Division Three (South).

SATURDAY 19TH NOVEMBER 1949

Fog caused the abandonment of Coventry's home game with Sheffield Wednesday. The crowd of 17,541 headed for home after 63 minutes when the whistle blew on proceedings. February saw the game replayed and City ran out 3-0 winners.

SATURDAY 19TH NOVEMBER 1977

Terry Yorath inspired the Sky Blues to a 4-1 victory over Queens Park Rangers at Highfield Road. Ian Wallace scored twice with a Mick Coop penalty completing the rout. Don Givens scored Rangers' consolation on a day when the two points took Coventry up to third in Division One. Over 20,000 watched City turn on the style as they would just miss out on a place in Europe.

SATURDAY 20TH NOVEMBER 1954

Ninth in the all-time Sky Blues appearance list, Roy Kirk scored the only goal in an FA Cup first-round win at the County Ground. His huge clearance from his own penalty area travelled 80 yards to bounce over the Cobblers' former City goalkeeper Alf Wood. Kirk made 349 first-team appearances between 1952 and 1959 and scored seven goals during this time.

THURSDAY 20TH NOVEMBER 1958

Ron Farmer made his Coventry debut against Chester City at Highfield Road. Signed in a double deal with Arthur Lightening from Nottingham Forest, Farmer played through all four divisions until his departure in October 1967. In total, he played 318 first-team matches and scored 52 goals from his wing-half role before transferring to Notts County. He served under Billy Frith, Jimmy Hill and Noel Cantwell and received a testimonial for his loyalty.

TUESDAY 20TH NOVEMBER 1973

The national power crisis ensured City sourced generators to enable the evening kick-off against Stoke City to go ahead. With a quarter-final place at stake in the League Cup, Coventry's floodlights needed assistance as the Sky Blues powered to a 2-1 win. Alan Green and Colin Stein cancelled out Geoff Hurst's opener in front of 17,434 supporters.

SKIPPER TERRY YORATH INSPIRED A 4-1 VICTORY OVER QUEENS PARK RANGERS

SATURDAY 21st NOVEMBER 1981

The Sky Blues' 5-2 defeat at Upton Park included a 20-minute delay when the floodlights failed. Steve Hunt gave City the advantage before West Ham raced into a 4-1 lead through Trevor Brooking, Jimmy Neighbour and two from Alvin Martin. Hunt made the scoreline respectable until Ray Stewart smashed home a late penalty.

SATURDAY 21st NOVEMBER 1992

Signed initially on loan from Newcastle United by Bobby Gould, Mick Quinn made his Sky Blues debut in a 3-2 home defeat to Manchester City. Quinn endeared himself to City supporters immediately as he scored twice to send Coventry into a 2-0 lead. Affectionately nicknamed 'Sumo' by the supporters, he went on to score in his first six matches and was soon signed permanently. Manchester City hit back to win 3-2 with goals from Mike Sheron, Fitzroy Simpson and a Keith Curle penalty but the Quinn legend had been born.

SATURDAY 22nd NOVEMBER 1930

Billy Lake scored twice as Coventry and Newport County found the back of the net ten times. Fortunately for City supporters, the cheers rang out six times as 8,276 watched the 6-4 victory at Highfield Road in the Division Three (South) clash.

TUESDAY 22nd NOVEMBER 1977

Mick Coop was rewarded for his loyalty to the Sky Blues with a testimonial match against a Scottish international side. Coop captained a Coventry City Great Britain XI and 8,000 supporters watched a 6-6 draw.

SATURDAY 23rd NOVEMBER 1940

Nine days after the devastating bombing of Coventry the *Midland Daily Telegraph* announced the closure of Highfield Road: "There will be no football at Highfield Road for a long time, Hitler having done a spot of ploughing up of the playing space with a series of bombs, besides knocking a large-sized hole in the new stand. In addition to that, no-one knows the exact whereabouts of the players. It is thought they are all safe but at the moment it is impossible to guarantee the raising of a team."

SATURDAY 24TH NOVEMBER 1934

Prior to the 7-0 thrashing of Macclesfield Town in 1999, Coventry recorded their biggest FA Cup victory with a 7-0 rout of Scunthorpe United at Highfield Road. Jock Lauderdale, Clarrie Bourton and Leslie Jones were amongst the scorers as City progressed to round two.

SATURDAY 24TH NOVEMBER 1973

The Sky Blues' Division One clash with Sheffield United kicked off at 2pm to enable the match to finish before darkness set in. Highfield Road watched Colin Stein and David Cross (two) seal a 3-1 win after Alan Woodward levelled on half-time. As mentioned previously, the national power crisis resulted in amended kick-off times years before Sky began changing schedules. Back in 1973, all kick-offs were 3pm and change was rare. Clubs had to be creative to enable their games to go ahead in the 'winter of discontent'.

SATURDAY 25TH NOVEMBER 1961

Billy Frith's final game of his second spell in charge of Coventry resulted in a calamitous 2-1 FA Cup first-round defeat at home to non-league Kings Lynn. City's goal even came courtesy of their visitors as they attempted to retrieve a two-goal half-time deficit. The City side that day included George Curtis, Brian and Peter Hill as 12,080 watched on in disbelief.

SATURDAY 25TH NOVEMBER 1972

Coventry led 1-0 at Portman Road when the floodlights failed with half an hour remaining. The match was abandoned and replayed ten days later when David Johnson and Trevor Whymark scored for Ipswich Town to drop City to ninth in Division One.

SATURDAY 25TH NOVEMBER 1995

Richard Shaw and Paul Williams both saw red as nine-man Coventry retrieved a 3-1 lead built up by the 'Crazy Gang' of Wimbledon. Vinnie Jones, Jon Goodman and Oyvind Leonhardsen scored for the Dons after Paul Heald's own goal had given City the lead. Dion Dublin gave the Sky Blues hope before David Rennie levelled at 3-3 with seven minutes remaining at Highfield Road.

TUESDAY 26TH NOVEMBER 1974

Bill Glazier's testimonial match at Highfield Road attracted 15,205 well wishers as Coventry drew 6-6 with an England World Cup side. Glazier himself scored twice against the legendary Gordon Banks as his loyal service was rewarded.

SATURDAY 26TH NOVEMBER 1977

Just seven days after a 4-1 thrashing of Queens Park Rangers took City third in Division One, they came crashing back down to earth at Goodison Park. Future Sky Blue Bob Latchford's hat-trick was aided by Martin Dobson, Jim Pearson and Andy King as the victory took Everton into second place. The 6-0 defeat was so out of character in Coventry's superb season which climaxed in a seventh-place finish.

WEDNESDAY 26TH NOVEMBER 1986

Coventry bowed out of the Littlewoods Cup in the fourth round up at Anfield. Jan Molby took the acclaim as he scored a hat-trick of penalties past Steve Ogrizovic to secure a 3-1 victory. Dave Bennett scored the Sky Blues goal on the hour.

SATURDAY 26TH NOVEMBER 1988

After 51 long years, Coventry finally beat Aston Villa in a league game. Cyrille Regis and Keith Houchen gave City a 2-0 lead and the last 15 minutes seemed like an eternity after Alan McInally's consolation for the visitors. Steve Sedgley picked up the Sky Blues' quickest-ever yellow card after just 14 seconds of a pulsating contest.

TUESDAY 27TH NOVEMBER 1962

Coventry won their FA Cup second-round replay against Millwall 2-1 at Highfield Road. Hubert Barr and Jimmy Whitehouse took the Sky Blues through to a third-round tie against Lincoln City.

SATURDAY 27TH NOVEMBER 1971

Francis Lee and Colin Bell shared four goals as Manchester City handed out a comprehensive defeat at Maine Road. The City side comprised Bill Glazier, Mick Coop, Geoff Strong, Wilf Smith, Jeff Blockley, Bobby Parker, Mick McGuire, Willie Carr, Chris Chilton, Ernie Hunt and Billy Rafferty.

WEDNESDAY 28TH NOVEMBER 1990

One of the best matches ever seen at Highfield Road took place on this day as Nottingham Forest visited the great stadium. Just 16,432 were present for the Rumbelows Cup fourth-round tie as Brian Clough's side trailed 4-0 after 35 minutes. Kevin Gallacher's hat-trick, and a Steve Livingstone strike, sent Sky Blues followers delirious until an amazing seven minutes from Nigel Clough reduced the deficit to 4-3 at half-time. Unbelievably, Garry Parker equalised for the East Midlands side before City regained their composure and Livingstone scored the winner on 62 minutes.

WEDNESDAY 29TH NOVEMBER 1961

Just four days after the Kings Lynn defeat, chairman Derrick Robins appointed Jimmy Hill as Coventry's new manager to replace Billy Frith. Hill left his job as chairman of the Professional Footballers' Association after four years and told the *Daily Mirror* just how he would go about his new role: "I'm going to be a hard man. My aim is to make Coventry the highest paid Football League club in the country, but you must work for it." Frith's backroom staff also departed in the cull and Hill sympathised: "It is unhappy for me that they should get the sack but soccer is a hard world." The tenth Coventry manager to leave the club since the war, Frith said: "I hadn't a clue about what was going on until I arrived at the ground this morning after returning from a reserve game at Brighton."

WEDNESDAY 29TH NOVEMBER 1961

In appointing Jimmy Hill as manager, chairman Derrick Robins instigated an extraordinary legacy that is still talked about today. Robins took over as chairman in October 1960 and his willingness to provide transfer funds to City's new manager paid dividends with two promotions. Robins was instrumental in the development of Highfield Road to prepare them for life in Division One as his vision reaped the rewards he'd hoped it would. Born in Bexley on the 27th June 1914, Robins left his post in April 1975 to move to South Africa as Gordon Milne's youth policy began to reap rewards. He sadly died on May 3rd 2004, aged 89, and a minute's silence was held prior to Peter Reid's first game in charge against Crystal Palace. As is commonplace nowadays, the silence gave way to thunderous applause in memory of Robins' tenure at Coventry City.

WEDNESDAY 29TH NOVEMBER 1995

Steve Ogrizovic saw red in the Coca Cola Cup fourth-round defeat at Wolverhampton Wanderers. City's 2-1 defeat saw Jonathan Gould replace Oggy and thus became the club's first-ever goalkeeping substitute as goals from Mark Venus and Darren Ferguson countered a Paul Williams consolation. Isaias made way for Gould as City sacrificed their midfield playmaker. Making his City debut was one-time Ghana sensation Nii Lamptey, a 16-year-old prodigy at Anderlecht in years gone by. He would make 11 first-team appearances, scoring twice, before moving on to Venezia in Italy.

SATURDAY 30TH NOVEMBER 1935

A year on from the 7-0 victory against Scunthorpe United in the FA Cup first-round tie, City drew them again at Highfield Road and had to settle for a replay after a 1-1 draw. Nine days later a Clarrie Bourton double was in vain as Coventry bowed out of the competition after a 4-2 replay defeat.

SATURDAY 30TH NOVEMBER 1963

George Hudson fired a hat-trick as the eventual Division Three champions smashed six goals past Queens Park Rangers at Loftus Road. Ken Hale, Willie Humphries and Ronnie Rees completed the 6-3 victory in front of 10,997 in west London. Hudson scored 24 goals in 32 league games before injury sidelined him. His replacement, George Kirby, scored five goals in nine games as the Sky Blues lifted the title.

SATURDAY 30TH NOVEMBER 1985

The previous away game ended Luton Town's unbeaten record on their artificial pitch. A fortnight later, City's squad packed their trainers for the journey to Loftus Road as they took on Queens Park Rangers. Terry Gibson, and a John Byrne own goal, saw the three points head back to the West Midlands in a season where the Sky Blues won only 11 matches all season as they avoided relegation by just two points. Lining up for the Astroturf specialists were Steve Ogrizovic, Brian Borrows, Greg Downs, David Bowman, Graham Rodger, Trevor Peake, Micky Adams, Wayne Turner, Cyrille Regis, Gibson and Dave Bennett as former City striker Gary Bannister led the Rangers attack.

COVENTRY CITY
On This Day

DECEMBER

TUESDAY 1st DECEMBER 1964

Leicester City travelled to Highfield Road for a League Cup fifth-round tie. In front of 27,443, George Hudson's strike was engulfed by no fewer than eight goals from City's Midland neighbours. In 1964, squad rotation had yet to be invented which made this result all the more extraordinary as Coventry fielded their first team. The result remains Leicester City's best-ever cup victory.

SATURDAY 1st DECEMBER 1979

FERGUSON 4 IPSWICH 1 read Highfield Road's electronic scoreboard after City's bearded number nine destroyed the Suffolk side. Up against Russell Osman and Kevin Beattie, Mick Ferguson had scored his goals by the 70th minute to leave John Wark's penalty scant consolation. Now in 2010, this remains the last time a Coventry player scored four goals in a league match. City's 4-1 victory was all the more impressive as their visitors would finish third in Division One and lay the foundations for their Uefa Cup triumph in 1981.

SATURDAY 2nd DECEMBER 1939

Harry Storer's men, in the newly formed Regional League Midland Division, visited Kenilworth Road to take on Luton Town. The Hatters smashed seven goals without reply but revenge would not be long in waiting. Three months later, City returned to Luton and won 5-1 with goals from Harry Barratt, Tom Crawley, and a hat-trick from Bobby Davidson.

FRIDAY 2nd DECEMBER 1960

Friday night football came to Coventry as Brentford visited under the floodlights. Just under 14,000 supporters watched Billy Myerscough score both goals as the new experiment worked well.

SATURDAY 2nd DECEMBER 1961

Jimmy Hill's first match as manager of Coventry City welcomed Northampton Town to Highfield Road. Mike Dixon's goal opened Hill's account and began an unbeaten run which stretched into the middle of March as City made their home ground a fortress. Hill's first season in Division Three ended with a 14th-place finish; the following year would see great strides made as the Sky Blues ended in fourth position.

SATURDAY 3RD DECEMBER 1966

Five months on from City's 3-1 win at Molineux, the same scoreline brought jubilation to Highfield Road as promoted Coventry closed in on the Division Two title. Back in December Ian Gibson, Ronnie Rees and John Key clinched two points for Jimmy Hill's men as 27,232 Black Country supporters watched the eventual champions at work.

SATURDAY 4TH DECEMBER 1926

St. James' Park, home of Exeter City, watched Coventry lose 8-1 in a Division Three (South) fixture. Jimmy Heathcote's goal in front of 5,000 supporters was one of 22 he scored during the season as City finished in 15th position.

SATURDAY 4TH DECEMBER 1982

Steve Whitton, whose opening goal in the 2-0 win over Brighton & Hove Albion was one of the best-ever seen at the old stadium, was born in East Ham. A product of the Sky Blues' youth policy, Whitton made his debut in September 1979 at home to Tottenham Hotspur in a 1-1 draw. Born on this day in 1961, Whitton celebrated his 21st birthday with a fabulous shot into the top corner of Perry Digweed's net as City went on to win 2-0. Disappointingly, only 8,035 were there to witness the goal on a cold and misty December day. During his four seasons in sky blue, Whitton made 72 first-team appearances and scored 23 goals, including 14 in 1982/83. This form prompted West Ham United to sign him in the summer exodus of 1983 and saw him play for the team he supported as a boy. After three seasons at Upton Park he moved on to Birmingham City, Sheffield Wednesday, Ipswich Town and Colchester United, making over 450 appearances.

MONDAY 4TH DECEMBER 1995

The Sky cameras picked a classic as Dion Dublin joined Terry Bly and David Speedie in scoring a hat-trick but still ending up on the losing side. Ron Atkinson's men led three times as Guy Whittingham, David Hirst, Marc Degryse, and finally Mark Bright, gave Sheffield Wednesday victory. City went so close to winning for the first time since August 23rd and slipped to 20th in the Premier League.

SATURDAY 5TH DECEMBER 1964

Rotherham United came away from Highfield Road with a 5-3 victory to increase the winless streak to six games. George Hudson, Ken Hale and Ken Keyworth's goals were in vain as the Millers smashed five past Bill Glazier in the Division Two clash.

MONDAY 6TH DECEMBER 1993

Mick Quinn's 79th-minute winner ensured City completed the double over the Gunners. Fellow striker Roy Wegerle was scathing in his after-match comments to the *Daily Mirror*: "You only need to take a look at Arsenal to see why England are struggling so badly. Half the Arsenal team were in Graham Taylor's squad, so it's no wonder England's displays began to reflect the fact that Arsenal aren't pulling up any trees these days." Quinn added his comments: "There is simply no way the Gunners could hope to win another title on this kind of form, or with this sort of football. Quite frankly, Paul Merson and Eddie McGoldrick were absolute passengers in the wide positions and their midfield was no better. They can forget any thoughts of winning the championship next season, never mind this." George Graham was livid: "Coventry had more desire than us and that's not good enough. Seaman had to rescue us far too often. We were non-existent in attack and I shall be making changes for the game against Spurs." Winding down the clock in the final moments, Sean Flynn took a clattering from Nigel Winterburn: "Fortunately, I saw Nigel coming at me out of the corner of my eye or otherwise I might have been badly hurt."

SATURDAY 6TH DECEMBER 1997

City's winless run at Villa Park continued as their hosts ran out easy 3-0 winners in front of 33,250. Stan Collymore, Lee Hendrie and future Sky Blue Julian Joachim, piled on the agony as the Sky Blues made it doubly difficult for themselves. Paul Williams and Gary Breen both saw red as City ended a forgettable match with nine men. Collymore's goal was his first for Villa in a game which saw Gavin Strachan make his City debut as substitute for Paul Telfer.

SUNDAY 6TH DECEMBER 2009

City's winless run at Glanford Park continued as Scunthorpe United took the three points in Sky's televised clash. Not quite a 'six pointer', the hosts capitalised on the Sky Blues' profligacy in front of goal to ensure it became nine games without a win. Gary Hooper's first-half strike past Keiren Westwood in front of the City away following proved if you don't take your chances at this level the opposition will punish you. It was hard to remember a match where Coventry wasted so many clear-cut opportunities.

SUNDAY 7TH DECEMBER 1958

Coventry goalkeeper Alf Wood became the oldest player to represent the club in the 3-1 FA Cup second-round tie defeat at home to Plymouth Argyle. Aged 43 years and 207 days, Wood made his debut for Coventry at the Vetch Field, home of Swansea City, in February 1938 aged 22. Following a spell at Northampton Town between 1951 and 1955, he returned to City as assistant trainer and, aside from his cameo return in the number one jersey in the autumn of 1958, left upon the arrival of Jimmy Hill. He made 246 first-team appearances between 1938 and 1958 before his place was taken by Arthur Lightening.

MONDAY 8TH DECEMBER 2003

Sky viewers witnessed a horrific accidental leg break as former City loanee Colin Healy was stretchered off in Gary McAllister's final game as a Sky Blues player. The points were shared with Stewart Downing's opener levelled by McAllister's penalty.

SATURDAY 9TH DECEMBER 1995

John Salako celebrated Coventry's second win of the season with their highest-ever Premier League victory. Blackburn Rovers, champions just seven months previous, were on the receiving end of a 5-0 rout on a snowy pitch at Highfield Road. Salako, who scored the fifth, spoke to the *Daily Mirror*: "We're over the moon with the result. We would have settled for one goal before the game but to score five was quite unbelievable. We were first to every loose ball and never let them get in the game. To outplay the champions like we did has given all of us a great boost."

WEDNESDAY 10TH DECEMBER 1980

After 97 years of trying, Gordon Milne's youngsters took the club to their first-ever semi-final. The 2-2 draw at Vicarage Road in the League Cup quarter-final preceded tonight's replay and Coventry scored five without reply in front of 30,389 vociferous supporters. West Ham United were the reward for a scintillating performance and Milne was ecstatic as he spoke to the *Daily Mirror*: "We won with a bit of style and that makes it even more enjoyable. We have got to be satisfied with this result and the way it was achieved." Chairman Jimmy Hill said: "This is the best result in my time at the club." While Watford manager Graham Taylor was gracious in defeat: "West Ham and Coventry will be evenly matched. I would not like to pick a winner in the semi-finals." On a glorious night, Mark Hateley (two), Peter Bodak, Garry Thompson and Steve Hunt scored City's goals against a Watford side who included future Sky Blues assistant manager Steve Harrison in their line-up.

SATURDAY 10TH DECEMBER 1983

Coventry C 4 Liverpool 0 beamed the scoreboard at Highfield Road. Unbelievable as it may seem, Bobby Gould's new recruits played the champions off the pitch with a wonderful performance. Nicky Platnauer headed home after just 45 seconds before Terry Gibson took centre stage as he took home the match ball after a show of deadly finishing past Bruce Grobbelaar.

SATURDAY 11TH DECEMBER 1982

It took Brian Roberts 192 first-team matches to score in Coventry colours. Upton Park was the venue as 'Harry' scored City's second in an impressive 3-0 win over the Hammers. Mark Hateley and Steve Whitton sandwiched Roberts' first goal of his career which he would add to just six weeks later at Highfield Road in a 2-2 FA Cup third-round tie against Norwich City. Sky Blues teammates made badges stating 'I saw Harry score' for a player who made 249 first-team appearances after joining the club from school in 1974. He moved to Birmingham City in the summer of 1984 for a fee of £10,000 before ending his career at Wolverhampton Wanderers.

SATURDAY 12TH DECEMBER 1931

Mansfield Town were on the receiving end of a 5-1 defeat at Highfield Road as Clarrie Bourton's four-goal haul gave him the match ball for the third time in 1931/32. John Cull completed the scoring as Harry Storer's free-scoring side continued to thrill.

SATURDAY 12TH DECEMBER 2009

Freddy Eastwood scored the first hat-trick at the Ricoh Arena as Chris Coleman's men beat bottom side Peterborough United 3-2. Craig Mackail-Smith's double had levelled at 2-2 before Eastwood smashed home a half volley to score the first treble since Lee Hughes in February 2002.

SATURDAY 13TH DECEMBER 1952

Eddie Brown and Don Dorman shared the match ball as Harry Storer's men thrashed Torquay United 7-2 at Highfield Road in the Division Three (South) fixture. Ronnie Waldock added to the trebles as City built on a spell of seven wins in eight games. The form would not continue as they finished sixth with a poor season-closing run of eight games without a win.

SATURDAY 13TH DECEMBER 1958

Greg Downs, who joined the Sky Blues from Norwich City, was born in Carlton, Nottinghamshire. Signed by Don Mackay, he made his debut at home to Manchester City on the opening day of season 1985/86 in a 1-1 draw. Over the course of the next five seasons, the hugely popular left-back appeared 182 times and scored seven goals. One of those strikes set the Sky Blues on the road to Wembley as he hammered home a free kick in the third-round tie against Bolton Wanderers. A member of the FA Cup-winning side, Downs moved to Birmingham City before winding down his career at Hereford United. After football, he moved back to Norfolk where he works as a policeman.

SATURDAY 14TH DECEMBER 1985

Don Mackay's men sank to 15th in Division One as Manchester City won 5-1 at Maine Road. Gordon Davies (two), Mark Lillis, Paul Simpson and a Graham Rodger own goal netted for the blue side of Manchester before Terry Gibson's late strike.

FRIDAY 14TH DECEMBER 2007

The club avoided administration by 30 minutes after Ray Ranson's SISU Capital consortium completed their takeover at the Ricoh Arena. Coventry had been given a 4 pm deadline to complete the deal or face a ten-point deduction. Outgoing chairman Joe Elliott was delighted to welcome Mr Ranson and SISU Capital to the club as he spoke to *The Times*: "This is a very exciting day in the long, proud history of Coventry City Football Club and I am positive that will be reflected in the attendance for the Southampton game. I am sure that Ray Ranson and SISU Capital will help drive Coventry City forward into a brand new era for the club. I'd like to thank the board and associate directors for their magnificent support and ask that remaining shareholders return their signed forms or attend the special office at the Ricoh Arena – as per the instructions within the shareholders' document – by Monday evening. I'd like to pay special thanks to Iain Dowie, his management team, the players and all the staff at Coventry City who have loyally supported the club through such a difficult time."

SATURDAY 15TH DECEMBER 1973

George Best scored his final goal for Manchester United as City travelled to the north-west and returned with two points. The win took Gordon Milne's men up to eighth as their prestigious opponents fell to 19th and would end the season in the relegation zone under Tommy Docherty. Colin Stein, Brian Alderson and David Cross each beat Alex Stepney as Best and Willie Morgan's strikes would prove to not be enough for the European champions of just six seasons previous.

SATURDAY 15TH DECEMBER 2007

Bradley Wright-Phillips cancelled out Jay Tabb's 19th-minute goal as 19,143 welcomed Ray Ranson and SISU Capital to the Ricoh Arena with a tumultuous reception. Manager Iain Dowie spoke to BBC Sport of his hopes now the takeover had been completed: "I always have a shopping list ready just like any manager. There are one or two areas we would like to look at and if we want to take this club forward we have to do that. The new chairman wants to sit down with me next week and he has said he wants to invest from the academy upwards and strengthen the first team."

SATURDAY 16TH DECEMBER 1967

Bobby Gould scored the Sky Blues' first hat-trick in the top flight as Burnley were beaten 5-1 at Highfield Road. Ronnie Rees and Ernie Machin added to Gould's trio as Andy Lochhead's late goal was a mere consolation. Just over 28,000 saw City's first win since the middle of September when they beat West Bromwich Albion 4-2.

SATURDAY 16TH DECEMBER 1978

There was drama shortly before kick off at The Dell as six Sky Blues players got stuck in a lift and needed to be rescued by the Southampton fire brigade. Sixth-place City never recovered from the disruption and lost 4-0, to a Saints side that included Alan Ball, Phil Boyer and Steve Williams, in front of 19,102 fans. There was also a rare occurrence as Mick Coop missed a late penalty, saved by Terry Gennoe.

SATURDAY 17TH DECEMBER 1960

Peter Hill opened the scoring for Billy Frith's men as Barnsley trooped away from Highfield Road on the receiving end of a 5-2 defeat. Ray Straw, Stewart Imlach, Ron Hewitt and an own goal, gave Coventry the two points. One-club man, Hill, born on August 8th 1931, played for City from 1948 to 1962 and amassed 309 first-team appearances before retiring in his early thirties. Only five other players have scored more goals in sky blue as Hill's 78 left him eight behind Frank Herbert and three ahead of George Hudson. Herbert scored his 86 goals in just 199 games having joined Coventry in 1922. He retired upon leaving City in 1929 and moved into the pub trade.

SATURDAY 17TH DECEMBER 1988

The floodlights were at it again as they delayed City's final score filtering through to the *Grandstand* vidiprinter by 19 minutes as City's home encounter with Derby County came to an unwelcome halt. Dean Saunders and Ted McMinn lit up a poor game with second-half goals to drop Coventry to fifth in the table under John Sillett.

SATURDAY 18TH DECEMBER 1937

Plymouth Argyle's 'Green Army' headed up the M5 for the Division Two clash at Highfield Road. Doubles from McPhee and McDonald sent Harry Storer's men to their third consecutive win as 21,511 fans saw a 4-0 home win. City ended the season in fourth position and would repeat the feat the following year.

SATURDAY 19TH DECEMBER 1992

"I just can't believe what is happening to me. It's like a dream come true," spoke Mick Quinn to the *Daily Mirror* shortly after Coventry thumped Liverpool 5-1 to send the City crowd home ecstatic with a fantastic display. "I've said all along that when Coventry won, they would win big – but to run up a scoreline like this against the club I idolised as a kid is so thrilling… I can't find the words." Manager Bobby Gould joked: "Quinn is fat and round but he's also phenomenal in the box which is why I could not wait to buy him." Rival boss Graeme Souness snapped: "We went to pieces in the end. This result has put the tin lid on one of the worst weeks of my life. Four decisions by referee Kelvin Morton changed the course of the game after we threatened to do to Coventry what they did to us." Brian Borrows (two) added to Quinn's double with Kevin Gallacher completing a fantastic victory.

WEDNESDAY 20TH DECEMBER 1933

Reg Matthews, the first Coventry City player to appear in a full international for England, was born in the city. Matthews made his England debut in 1956 against Scotland at Hampden Park and went on to win five caps in total. In 1956, City were in Division Three (South) so his achievement is all the greater based on where he was playing league football at the time. After 116 appearances for the club, Matthews moved to Chelsea, then in Division One, for a fee of £22,500 which stood as a record transfer fee for a goalkeeper at the time. After a further five seasons on the Kings Road, Derby County signed him and he went on to make nearly 250 appearances for the Rams before retiring in 1968. Reg Matthews sadly died on October 7th 2001, aged 67.

TUESDAY 20TH DECEMBER 1960

Fourth in the all time appearance list, Brian Borrows was born in Liverpool. During his City career he played 488 first team games and scored 13 goals from his right back position. One of Coventry's most consistent performers over 12 seasons from 1985 onwards, Borrows made the position his own but sadly missed out on the Wembley final after suffering a knee injury. He moved on to Swindon Town for two seasons before taking on coaching roles back at Coventry.

SATURDAY 21ST DECEMBER 2002

Happily for the main bulk of the 13,185 on a bitterly cold day at Highfield Road, this time the streaker was female as a young lady made her way from the West Terrace to plant a smacker on Mo Konjic. Sky cameras were present to watch City win 3-0 against Derby County and viewers were treated to two spectacular strikes from Gary McAllister and on loan Craig Hignett. Hignett played only nine times and scored twice as his arrival coincided with four straight wins. Seven days after this match he was injured and sent back to parent club Middlesbrough. City went on to win just one of their final 21 matches, against Grimsby Town, recently relegated out of the Football League.

SATURDAY 22ND DECEMBER 1962

Dense fog led to the abandonment of the home fixture against Colchester United. Jimmy Hill, prior to kick off, had led supporters in a practice rendition of the new Sky Blues song, written to the tune of the Eton Boating Song. At half-time there was hope the fog would lift so Hill went back onto the pitch during the extended interval for a few more renditions of the new chorus. With City leading 2-0 the referee decided to abandon the fixture but how ironic that John Sillett and George Curtis, in the City line up this day, would witness the loudest rendition of all at Wembley in 1987.

SATURDAY 22ND DECEMBER 2007

On this day, now Premier League Blackpool won 4-0 at Bloomfield Road in front of 8,690 fans. Of the City starting eleven, only Ben Turner and Michael Doyle are still with the club.

SUNDAY 23RD DECEMBER 1962

Terry Gibson, signed by Bobby Gould from Tottenham Hotspur in the summer of 1983, was born in Walthamstow. Just 5ft 4in tall, the 20-year-old terrorised Division One defences in his three seasons in sky blue and scored 52 goals in only 113 appearances. During his City career, Gibson played alongside Dave Bamber, Graham Withey, Mick Ferguson, Bob Latchford and Cyrille Regis but still the goals flowed. He scored on his debut against Watford at Vicarage Road and famously scored a hat-trick in the 4-0 win over Liverpool. His final City appearance in January 1986 saw City draw 3-3 with Aston Villa, after which he was sold to Manchester United for £650,000 in a swap with Alan Brazil. Reunited with Bobby Gould at Wimbledon, he won an FA Cup winners' medal in the 1-0 victory over Liverpool. He looks back fondly over his time at Coventry: "When I came to Ryton to discuss my move there were only six first team players training. Bob was like a Sunday League manager trying to put a side together. I only met Micky Gynn at Watford before the first game. We were all strangers to each other but we all had something to prove."

SATURDAY 24TH DECEMBER 1955

Coventry have played just six times on Christmas Eve, the last match in 1955 welcomed Norwich City to Highfield Road as City ran out 5-3 winners. The late Charlie Timmins was amongst the scorers in the Division Three (South) clash. Between 1949 and 1958 he played 165 first-team games under six different managers and his only goal came on this day. He sadly died on April 13th 2010, and upon the announcement at the Ricoh Arena there was warm applause from old and new supporters.

WEDNESDAY 25TH DECEMBER 1918

Harry Barratt, who made 178 first-team appearances and scored 13 goals, was born in Headington. He spent his entire professional career with Coventry and made his debut in a 3-2 win over Blackburn Rovers at Highfield Road. World War II interrupted his career at City and upon retiring in 1952 he went on to manage Gillingham in the late 1950s for four seasons. In 1989 he sadly died, aged 71.

TUESDAY 25TH DECEMBER 1956

Just three days after the home fixture against Crystal Palace was abandoned at 0-0 after a floodlight failure, blizzards put paid to the away fixture at Newport County on Christmas Day. The referee called a halt after 71 minutes with visibility poor and conditions worsening.

FRIDAY 25TH DECEMBER 1959

The last game to be played on Christmas Day saw Ken Satchwell score four times in the 5-3 win against Wrexham. During the game, City full-back Mick Kearns stepped back to launch a long throw and fell over the surrounding pitch wall. He returned, bandaged, with stitches applied in the days prior to substitutions. One day later City travelled to Wrexham for their next league game and won 3-1.

WEDNESDAY 26TH DECEMBER 1984

Bobby Gould's final match in his first spell as manager ended in a 2-0 defeat at Kenilworth Road. Brian Stein and Ray Daniel scored for Luton Town in their final season on grass prior to the 'plastic pitch' installation.

SUNDAY 26TH DECEMBER 1999

One of Highfield Road's best games saw both Arsenal and the Sky cameras visit. Sublime strikes from Gary McAllister, Moustapha Hadji and Robbie Keane were replied to by Freddie Ljungberg and Davor Šuker but City held on to take the three points. Manager Gordon Strachan was delighted as he spoke to the *Daily Mirror*: "There was no luck in our goals today. We were the better side against a top team who had almost all of their first choice players playing." Making his debut as substitute for the Sky Blues was Swedish right-back Tomas Gustafsson. Halfway through his three-year spell at City he changed his surname to Antonelius as apparently Gustafsson is very common in Sweden – so he switched to his sister's married name. His stay was fairly unproductive and he played just 18 times for the first team before moving to FC Copenhagen. Following retirement in September 2003 he went to university and studied Economics. While at Coventry he added to his Swedish international caps, along with Magnus Hedman, and collected ten in total.

TUESDAY 27TH DECEMBER 1977

Just one day after Graham Oakey was carried off the Villa Park pitch to never play in City's colours again, the Sky Blues and Norwich City served up a nine-goal feast for 21,609 fans. The Canaries led 3-2 at half-time having trailed to goals by Barry Powell and Ian Wallace. Ray Gooding and Bobby McDonald took City into a 4-3 lead before World Cup winner Martin Peters levelled with 15 minutes on the clock. There was more drama to follow as Ray Graydon made the score 5-4 before John Ryan's last-minute penalty was clawed away by Jim Blyth.

SATURDAY 27TH DECEMBER 1980

Sky Blues' number nine Mark Hateley scored his first league goal of the season in the 2-2 draw at Stoke City's Victoria Ground. It would take him until the middle of January to score his first home league goal in the 1-1 draw with Aston Villa.

SATURDAY 27TH DECEMBER 1986

More fireworks on December 27th as Tottenham Hotspur turned up without their change strip and wore City's yellow away kit. Another memorable match held the drama until the final minute when Cyrille Regis soared to plant a header past Ray Clemence to soak up the adulation of the West Stand. Keith Houchen and Dave Bennett (two) scored earlier in the game in reply to goal machine Clive Allen (two) and Nico Claesen. Over 22,000 were treated to end-to-end football as City moved up three places to seventh.

TUESDAY 28TH DECEMBER 1982

Young right-back Peter Hormantschuk's long-range shot bounced through the arms of Manchester United's goalkeeper Gary Bailey as City were on their way to a 3-0 victory at Highfield Road. Mark Hateley and Jim Melrose added to the strike in a Red Devils performance that infuriated Ron Atkinson. Speaking to the *Daily Mirror* he said: "This was a hotch-potch of a performance. One or two players will have to get their fingers out. Yet give Coventry credit, they made life difficult for us."

SUNDAY 28TH DECEMBER 1997

With four minutes remaining, Coventry trailed Manchester United 2-1 at Highfield Road. Enter Darren Huckerby as his twisting run resulted in a penalty converted by Dion Dublin. Straight from the visitors' kick off, he collected the Goal of The Month award with a memorable slalom through United's back line to slot the ball home. The highest crowd of the season, 23,055, watched in amazement as the Sky Blues fought back to take the three points.

MONDAY 29TH DECEMBER 1997

Newspapers the next day headlined Coventry's performance. Huckerby was elated as he spoke to the *Daily Mirror*: "I guess you would have to say that's the best goal I've ever scored. I don't remember much about it, apart from the impression of leaving a string of United bodies behind me. I never saw their faces."

SATURDAY 30TH DECEMBER 1933

Arthur Bacon scored five times as Coventry beat Gillingham 7-3 at the Priestfield Stadium. Apart from Cyrille Regis and Clarrie Bourton, no other City player has achieved the feat.

MONDAY 30TH DECEMBER 1974

It is fair to say Noel Whelan was one of the most colourful characters to wear sky blue in recent years. Born in Leeds on this day, Ron Atkinson signed him from Leeds United for £2 million in December 1995. Whelan marked his home debut with a wonderful goal as City beat Everton 2-1 and went on to score 39 goals in 156 first-team appearances before moving to Middlesbrough in the summer of 2000.

SATURDAY 31ST DECEMBER 1966

Jimmy Hill's promotion-in-waiting side ended 1966 with a 5-1 thrashing of Portsmouth. Highfield Road watched Bobby Gould, John Tudor, Ernie Machin, John Key and John Mitten continue the club's unbeaten run which would stretch to 25 matches. City remained unbeaten from November 26th until the end of the season. Their next defeat came on the opening day of their top-flight sojourn, 2-1 at Burnley's Turf Moor in August 1967.